Me,
My Podium
and I

Me, My Podium and I

JOHN JAMES COOPER

The author may be contacted at jjcooper39@hotmail.com

EP&J2 PUBLISHING
Cookeville, Tennessee

ISBN Paperback: 978-1-7355600-3-8
ISBN eBook: 978-1-7355600-4-5

Library of Congress Control Number: 2022913036

This book is dedicated to my stepson, Jared Allen Galloway,
whom I aspire to be like when I grow up.

Contents

Introduction

I have always been a person who enjoys his own company. When I am alone, I do not feel alone. *Loneliness*, that thing that many spend their lives trying to avoid, is a friend to me. He does, at times, force me to exclude all others so that we can enjoy, undisturbed, the vast and exciting workings of my mind. Some have accused my good friend of having a dark nature. That is true but only because of his startling ability to see things as they really are. His vision is not obscured by that glitter-coated optimism, which is so common among the masses. Within the confines of my mind, Loneliness and I have conversations without end as we constantly question everything, including our own beliefs. Possible answers are researched and analyzed, and if solutions exist, they are eventually found. Finding answers to seemingly unanswerable questions gives us great joy. But our favorite entertainment is rhetoric. We love to develop persuasive arguments against all the silliness we see in the world. We take great pleasure in pointing out contradictions or truths that simply are not truths but are still blindly followed by the majority of folks. In the very center of my mind stands a podium from which I present my arguments. My presentations are so passionate yet so logical that I am convinced I will someday be named one of the great orators. This from a man who can't have a conversation with another person without fumbling over words. Oh well, no harm in dreaming.

When I have spent too much time alone with my friend Loneliness, my wife will politely remind me that it is time for lunch or supper. Sometimes, being a bit more direct, she will tell me that I have been piddling around with my thoughts long enough and that I need to tune back into the "here and now" channel. Thank goodness there is just enough room in my life for a tolerant and forgiving spouse. She is a godsend. Without her, I am sure I would seldom get out of my own head.

Now, here's the thing. If you read the above and understood it, better yet could even relate to it, then you are an introvert, possibly a recluse. Either way, this little book is for you. On the other hand, if you read the above and it made no sense to you whatsoever, then this little book is not for you. Pass it on to a friend with a more appropriate disposition.

Because I have spent much of my life alone, I have begun to wonder if I am "special," you know, odd . . . eccentric . . . unstable. I am not a people person, so I have seldom shared my thoughts with others. Over the span of my life, I have tried once or twice. On those few occasions, people listened attentively for a minute or two. Then they would stare at me as if they didn't understand, couldn't come up with an appropriate response, or, perhaps, thought I was speaking in a language other than their own. Early on my wife clearly informed me that she "didn't get it," nor did she want to "get it." She thought it was best if I kept "it" in my room between myself and whomever it was that I frequently mumbled to.

So, I have put this collection of random thoughts in print and have released it on the public in the form of this small book. Hopefully, someone will understand. I need to know if there are others out there like me. Any comments or sharing of thoughts would be greatly appreciated. Responses can be addressed to jjcooper39@hotmail.com.

Please be forewarned. These essays address matters that may be considered sensitive to some readers and will challenge the beliefs of others. They do not represent my final opinion but rather my observations of life. Proceed with caution.

The Death of a Superhero

I was a superhero, and so were my friends. I clearly remember how we would save the world from destruction, oftentimes more than once, before we were marshaled off the school bus and herded into our cellblocks (a.k.a. classrooms). In mid-afternoon, we escaped from our routine incarceration at the local institution of learning. After a halfhearted but sufficient effort at our homework, we were free to rescue at least a few fair damsels from their distress, prevent an alien invasion, and maybe even have time to outwit, outsail, outfight an armada of pirates (possibly capturing Blackbeard himself). All this was usually accomplished by the time we were reeled in from our fantasies by familiar voices telling us it was time to wash up and eat supper. This went on for years, and we were pretty sure that the world had no chance of survival without our heroic efforts. We had gained our superpowers long before we started school and held on to them, to a certain degree, far into our junior high years. Adults, especially our parents, used to appreciate us flying through the living room with our capes, which were made from threadbare towels and waved wildly in our wake. But times changed, and eventually we were ignored, then ridiculed, and then sternly reminded of our age.

By the time we reached fourteen or fifteen, our brains had been washed nearly clean of any make-believe. Though, from time to time, even into our late teens, we did stare out classroom windows, daydreaming. We dreamed of possessing special powers and extraordinary talents, performing acts of bravery, or achieving the unachievable, all in some instinctual effort to feel special, to hold on to our uniqueness, to fight off a foreboding of becoming ordinary. But these daydreams were only remnants of the fantasies that we had experienced during our earlier years. In the end, it was our unavoidable exposure to education, religious ideologies, and all the other aspects of socialization that overwhelmed us and had a profound effect on us that proved irreversible. This slow, methodical process of pressurization was used to force us into adult reality. And it was that reality that stifled, then strangled, the life out of our youthful spontaneity and prolific imaginations. It turned out that adult reality was our kryptonite, and it slowly killed the superhero, the exceptional part that lived inside of us. Despite our best efforts, we could not avoid being force-fed, spoonful after spoonful, our daily dose of what *they* said was real and what was not. The belief in and even the memory of our superhero status faded, and so did our superpowers.

One day we woke no longer able to fly. Our wings had been clipped, and we found ourselves living in the cramped quarters of a tiny cage that was constructed of enforced expectations, appropriate limitations, social responsibility, and demands for conformity. We would occasionally exert a genuine effort to summon up and use our old powers to break free, but to no avail. That cage was constructed of that damnable kryptonite, that fucking adult reality, and there was no escaping it.

Now, as an old man, I spend a good portion of my time doing what old men tend to do: observing and reflecting on life rather than participating in it. And occasionally, even in my dotage, I find myself drifting off into a daydream of sorts. The difference now is that I daydream about what I could have been, as my time remaining is too short to be wasted on wondering what I might become. And even though I have only the faintest remembrance of what it was like to be a superhero, I still possess that old desire to feel special. That desire was the prime incentive for creating the hero in me, and though it now flickers, as if exhausted by age, it has not burned out.

I like to think that someone will remember me a little longer than the few months it typically takes for folks to shake off the memory of those who have passed. Motivated by some peculiar anxiety, I desperately try to think of something special about myself, my life, my achievements . . . hell, even an outstanding failure would do if it could help the memory of me persist a little while longer once I am gone. But this desperate search is all for naught. My chance to be special enough to be remembered was lost long ago when my superhero status was stolen right out from under me. When that theft occurred, an anger took up residence in my being. It grew to become a darkness, like a shadowy extension of myself that constantly tried to take full possession of me. There were times when I became weary of resisting, and it would overcome me. I would spend days in a rage that had no particular target and only resulted in making my life even more wretched. Finally, I decided it was best to make friends with this piece of myself before it killed me. I discovered that the anger at the root of it all was part of a grieving process that had gotten stuck and never resolved itself. I was still grieving the tremendous loss of my fantastic fantasy world where my belief in my greatness made me great, made me special. I am still angry, even today, over that loss. I am angry at myself for having not been smart enough or strong enough to hold on to at least a small portion of just one of my superpowers. If I had, I would now once again be able to stand proud, my hands on my hips and my chest out. Perhaps I would still be wearing an old T-shirt, one size too small, hidden under my daily attire, with a symbol or letter drawn on it in magic marker. It would remind me of my specialness. And I am sure there would be a glow around me, an aura that only surrounds special people, people who are proud of themselves and of their achievements. But no. Because my superpowers made others uncomfortable, I changed. I was weak and stupid, so I conformed to please others, others who had no understanding or appreciation of who I was and the potential I possessed. I chose to fit in, to be accepted rather than to be myself. I gave up my powers along with my treasured hero status and became one of the many who then stumbled through life sedated by the mediocrity of their ordinary existence.

I have recently come to a place in life where I fear living too long much more than I fear death. I am caught up in the inescapable spiral of rapid physical decomposition that signals the final stage of this life cycle. Let me assure you, the shedding of this mortal shell is an unpleasant and painful experience. So much so that I recently found myself at a hardware store checking the weight capacity of various ropes and searching about in my room for a sturdy, exposed beam. But before I decided to kick a chair out from under myself, I thought: why don't you get off your lazy ass and do something to distract yourself from all this physical pain and from that worrisome thought of death? You can always get back to ending it a little later if you still feel the need. Motivated by these thoughts, I have taken up that time-honored activity referred to as *people watching*. I am especially drawn to observing the younger folks, particularly young families going about their daily lives. This gets me out of my dismal living quarters and proves to be a good way to occupy myself while I await my pending finale. By the way, in case you are not aware, Death is one inconsiderate son-of-a-bitch who seldom shows up when he's expected. He is obviously a mischievous fucker in that he takes the greatest pleasure in showing up when you are not ready or not showing up when you are. All the inconvenience and worry that his unpredictability causes could be avoided if he would just keep to a schedule.

Anyway, there is a small park, not far from where I live. It only covers the space of a city block, maybe two. And though it is not well kept, it still attracts many locals as it is the only option in the immediate area for getting some semi-fresh air. It has become my habit to go to the park most days, weather permitting. These outings to a public area require some preparatory tasks, many of which I normally wouldn't be bothered with. I must give myself a good birdbath when it's in between my infrequent showers so as not to risk offending the delicate sensibilities of those who frequent the park. My hair is long and unruly. I comb it back, trying not to look too much like a madman. Shaving is just too much of a task, but I do, usually, attend to it on bath days. I do not give my shirt much thought since I wear a coat everywhere I go. I change my pants, but only if the food stains are so bad I think they might draw attention. I do change my underwear if they have shit stains or if they are yellowed due to my occasional incontinence. I put on two pair of socks, no matter the season, being that my feet are always cold. I carry no wallet because I have nothing to put in a wallet. If I do happen to have a few dollars, I shove them into my socks, as it is not safe to leave anything of value in the room.

In my neighborhood, it is necessary to carry some type of personal protection. This area is infested with cowardly hooligans who, for profit and sport, attack anyone who appears defenseless. In one coat pocket I carry mace, and in the other an old pocket pistol. I have never fired the pistol, but I have used the mace a few times—once to prevent my groceries from being stolen and once to protect a bit of pocket change I mistakenly exposed when I was paying for a Little Debbie and a soda pop. I am always sure to grab my hand-carved walking stick. It is my prized possession, a gift from my only friend (my brother), who died some years ago. I call it Old Hickory—I bet you can guess why. It serves many purposes, such as fending off ill-tempered dogs and ill-mannered children, but most importantly it provides support for my trip back from the park. It always seems easier to get there than it is to get back.

I can't help but notice a group of parents, five or six in number, who apparently know each other and routinely meet here at the park with their children. They seem to share a similar philosophy related to child rearing, as they all have the same habit of interacting with their little children as if they were little adults. These kids are old enough to have gotten a good grip on basic language skills. Some of them are a little older and a little more advanced. It is obvious that these parents equate language skills with the existence of advanced intellect. They seem to be working under the misconception that the more a child sounds like an adult, the more they should be treated as an adult. At first, I think that these young mothers and fathers have somehow overlooked the fact that language skills are a tool to assist in the development of advanced intellect and not the manifestation of an advanced intellect. But how could this be with so much available information related to child development and the facts of brain growth and function being the most basic of textbook information? It is as if they have convinced themselves that by some miraculous means their offspring, while still in the body of a wee child, have come into possession of a fully developed adult brain. Once you start believing in some strange shit like that, your mind tends to grab on to anything that supports your delusion and disregard even the most blatant facts that do not. For example, a child's efforts to please by mimicking whatever they hear their parents say only serves to reinforce these parents' belief that the child is communicating with them on some sophisticated level. All the while, they ignore the fact that the child cannot offer even the slightest rationale for what they are regurgitating.

It is worth noting that this constant repeating of someone else's ideas and beliefs presents a real threat to the child's chance of becoming the unique individual they are meant to be. Ideologies forced on the child during their impressionable years easily become fixed beliefs on major life issues. Views on morality, race, education, religion, politics, and life's purpose can all be instilled in the child long before they have the mental tools to make decisions on their own. And even though young adults often take pride in claiming that they have thrown off their parents' old beliefs, they most often have only made some small alteration to what was pounded into their brains during childhood. In other words, these children are being programmed to believe versus being allowed the time and freedom to choose what to believe.

The ability to develop language skills occurs around the same time that a child's imagination is fully awakened. And here is where the real crimes are being committed. These parents who frequent the park routinely deliver crushing verbal blows to their own children in a most obvious effort to destroy the child's imagination and to force the child to accept their parents' belief system, their parents' adult reality. One parent uses threats of corporal punishment saying, "Didn't I tell you to stop carrying that stuffed animal around with you? Are you talking to that thing again? Boy, I'm going to wear you out if you keep it up!" Another ridicules, "This is the last time you are wearing that worn-out cowboy costume. You look ridiculous. Do you want people to think something is wrong with you?" Another uses a softer tone to lessen the blow, but still kicks the child in the face with adult reality and says, "No, no, honey, there is no Santa Claus. I've told you that a hundred times. Don't you remember? It is your father and I who buy those gifts you find under the tree. I know you are still very young, but it is best to stop believing in such nonsense and start facing facts." These wolves in caregivers' clothing tear away at their child's imagination with no concern that they are disrupting a most necessary part of childhood development.

The collateral benefits of allowing, better yet encouraging, a child's imagination are numerous but often go unnoticed and unappreciated. Can we even begin to count all the skills that are being refined when children are engaged in the endless scenarios that they create in their minds? Coming up with complex alternative realities and then developing the methods and the tools to exist in such realities are not easy tasks. Planning, analyzing, executing, evaluating, problem solving—all the key features of critical thinking, not to mention the all-important task of character building—are occurring during this invaluable developmental period. It is during this time that the child discovers their strengths and weaknesses and starts the process of enhancing the former and compensating for the latter. They identify characteristics of the *good guy* and the *bad guy* (who often play major roles in their fantasies) and begin to incorporate the positive in their personal constitution and, hopefully, reject the negative. In addition, by giving free rein to the brain's limitless creativity, a sifting through of numerous possible talents occurs, allowing the child to find their unique aptitudes. Collectively, these have the potential for identifying the individual's direction and purpose in life. It is by way of these processes that the child becomes the special person they are supposed to be.

I observe these parents kicking the shit out of their children's imaginations, day after day, week after week. The things I hear them saying to their children reverberate in my head, eventually shaking the shackles off ancient memories. Once freed, these memories slam into my consciousness. They force me to recognize and acknowledge that I am observing the same sinister process that crushed my own childhood imagination, stole my superpowers, and murdered the superhero that had lived inside of me. That process destroyed any hope of me becoming the special person I was intended to be and condemned me to an existence that had no meaning to me and little to anyone else. With this realization, my duty becomes obvious. I had not been brave enough, strong enough, or smart enough to save myself when I was a child. But now, here is my chance to compensate for my past weaknesses, to redeem myself by perhaps saving at least a few of the little ones from these bastards who call themselves parents.

All of this crystallizes in a single moment of clarity as I sit in the park, no more than ten or fifteen feet from this group of perpetrators. One of the women has volunteered to supervise all the children in a play area not far away but far enough. The rest of the parents are huddled together, gossiping about some shit. I feel myself, in a rather robotic manner, stand up and take a few steps toward them. The first shot from my pocket pistol puts down the mother who threatened her child with corporal punishments. That shot startles the other park visitors. The second shot follows immediately but only incapacitates the target. That shot causes everyone to scatter. But still, I am able to bring down two more of the culprits before they can escape. Then my pistol clicks, then clicks again. I must have missed and wasted the other shots. The wounded parent is lying by a bench, bleeding out. I turn him over, and he looks at me as if surprised and asks, "Why?" I do not bother to answer; the guilty always know their sins. I get the best grip I can on Old Hickory, raise it above my head, and using every ounce of strength I can muster I strike him repeatedly. I must say that hickory wood lives up to its reputation of being a strong and durable material. The walking stick easily cracks the skull of that thieving murderer. By this time, many of those who had been in the park have found cover. But a considerable number of them are standing around the perimeter, as if frozen by some morbid curiosity, watching as events unfold. They stare at me as I stare at them. It is weird and unnerving, so I leave the park to them and go on about my business.

Supported by Old Hickory, I make my way back to my shitty room in that shithole of a boarding house. I am in no hurry to get there. I stop along the way to watch a murder of crows going through the contents of a trash bag someone had set out. I am exhausted when I close the door behind me. I want to lie down and rest for a few minutes. Just as I drift off, I am awakened by a commotion outside my window. I suppose those busybodies from the park have reported me to the authorities. Residents from my building are standing out in the street with a couple of officers and pointing out the location of my room.

People are gathering en masse, all hoping to see something more fucked-up than their own lives so they can feel better about themselves. They are motivated by that ugly part of humanity that takes pleasure in the troubles and suffering of others. Within minutes, more police arrive, blocking off the road and taking up strategic positions. Then I see a SWAT vehicle pull up, and I think to myself, what a waste of resources. You would think they were preparing to extract an entire terrorist organization instead of one senior citizen who had simply done his duty to prevent villainous characters from committing felonies against little children. As the police negotiator calls for me to come outside so we can *just talk,* the thought crosses my mind that maybe I should try to explain. But I know there is little chance they will understand, and even if they do, what difference will it make? Besides, I am simply too tired to try.

Suddenly my mind lands on a profound realization. I have finally done something special. I have become a hero by saving those children from the same horrible fate I had suffered. What more is left for me to do with the little time I have remaining? Hell, that little bit of time would now be spent in some prison with a bunch of half-wits who I can only hope don't have some sick sexual obsession that involves turning an old guy into their bitch. But even if all this wasn't so, there is still little reason to go on. I have no one to care for or to live for. I assure you; this is not by choice. I did try to find a companion until the desire finally faded away, but I never had any luck coming across anyone who wanted to be with someone who was no one. Too, this merciless aging process has made my daily existence a misery by wreaking havoc on all my bodily systems. My life is totally void of any pleasure. I used to enjoy the occasional excess intake of spirits, but no more. Now even a single shot of liquor sets off a blazing heartburn that feels like the devil has shoved a flaming brimstone down my throat and inserted it into the center of my chest. There is no hope of ever experiencing sexual satisfaction again. Even the most persistent and experienced sex worker cannot cause my flaccid member to pay attention—they have tried. I no longer enjoy my food since my taste buds have withered and died. My olfactory nerves have disconnected from my brain, evidenced by the fact that I often become aware that I have soiled myself only because of the expression on someone's face as I pass them in the hallway. Then there are those periods of constipation when taking a shit is only accomplished by a Herculean effort that involves straining, sweating, and the offering up of prayers and promises to God (none of which I intend on keeping). My bladder has become a little rascal who likes to surprise me by emptying itself without any warning. And due to arthritis, I go to bed each night feeling like I have been in a major automobile accident and wake up feeling the same. I could go on and on, but you get the picture. And we all know that this will only get worse and worse. When I consider the situation, I see a lot of reasons to be done with this sad-ass life and none to continue it.

I put my coat back on, mace in one pocket and that empty pocket pistol in the other. I grab my walking stick, then remember that it is not safe to leave anything of value in the room. I check my socks to be sure my few dollars are still there. They are. I trudge on down the hallway and step out onto the front stoop. There is a frenzy of activity as officers pull their weapons and take cover. I feel Old Hickory pressing into my hand. I am so tired that I am not sure if I can even stand without my old friend supporting me. I find solace in knowing that Old Hickory will end up secured away in a police evidence locker, protected from those who would not understand its value. The negotiator has been pulled back, and a cocky young officer standing behind his squad car shouts out, "Let's see your hands, old man, both of them." I close my eyes and think about the children I have saved today as l pull the empty pistol out of my pocket.

The bullets hitting, then ripping, through my body feel like someone punching me with their fists. Shock sets in almost immediately, making me numb to any real pain. In that stunned state, staring up at the sky, I swear I see my childhood self flying up and away with that cape, made from a threadbare towel, waving in my wake. I smile as I watch myself performing various aerobatics, not even noticing the darkness that slowly closes in around me like a warm embrace until it finally engulfs the little that remains of me.

Social Imperative

When I was a child, I was blissfully unaware of the social change that raged around me. My innocence was my protection from the frightful realities of this world.

When I was a young man, I was a part of social change. But, somehow, I was oblivious to the profound impact my lackadaisical involvement was having on the society that I lived in. It wasn't until much later in life that I realized my halfhearted participation and my sometimes total lack of participation were in fact the most destructive forms of participation.

When I was middle-aged, my social and political views had solidified, causing me to believe, naively, that society should conform to my beliefs. I was sorely disappointed when it did not.

When I was older, I simply wanted social change to stop. I was hoping that if it would, a remnant of something familiar might be preserved so that I did not feel so much like a foreigner in my own country. But my hope was in vain; change is a force that cares not for the wants or wishes of any man.

Now that I am old, I realize that social change began with the birth of civilization. It is an inexorable force that built then eroded away all empires and nations of the past, no matter how great, no matter how powerful they may have been. That force continues today and will continue into perpetuity to create and destroy nations across the globe.

It created and is now in the process of eroding what we know as the United States of America. We are all witness to this destruction, but because our lifespans are so short, we tend to view this insidious dismantling of our society as just singular events that are harmless and unrelated. We are unable to see that these events are snippets of a continuous process, a chipping away, that over time will result in the end of this particular way of life. This will happen for no reason other than the fact that we are driven by that social imperative, *change*, which dictates that nothing can last as it is forever.

We could discuss the possible origin of this imperative. But that would be as futile as trying to track down the answer to what sparked the start of life. If we knew its origin, what would it matter? Time might be better spent figuring out why we are not able to learn from the abundance of documented history, accumulated over thousands of years, which provides irrefutable evidence that we build nations only so that we can destroy them. Why are we not able to acknowledge and alter that seemingly obvious self-destructive compulsion? It is as if we are totally blind to that propensity. This suggests there is a flaw in the workings of our intellect, bringing into question not only our general capacity to learn from experiences but too our abilities of self-examination and self-determination.

I fear that the desire to create, then to destroy, is so tightly woven into our being that it is impossible to extract it from ourselves. This pattern, which demands unending change, is simply an intrinsic truth of our existence, just as it is with all of Nature. And yes, we are a part of that macrocosm, although we seldom think of ourselves as such. But when we do, a certain logic reveals itself. We, as a part of Nature, are driven by the same force that drives Nature. That force is change, and change is time manifested. If change stops, time stops. I think that our need for change, realized in our pattern of creation and destruction, is really just a part of an instinct to survive—to keep time going.

When it comes to the more immediate reality of social change, you can only hope that you are not around when your way of life, the society you have known, finally deteriorates to the point that it literally ends. This has and will continue to occur on a global scale as nations rise and fall, with entire populations waking to new realities that they never allowed themselves to imagine.

Social change is also experienced on a smaller scale that is much more individual and intimate. In recent history, social change has been occurring at such a rapid rate that it is nothing short of phenomenal, but it is not so rapid that we are able to witness the destruction of a well-established nation in one lifetime. That still commonly requires centuries. But it is fair to say that, in a matter of a few generations, the society that a person is born into is likely to be transformed into an alien landscape. People, all people, as they reach the age of sixty or so, if not before, become wide-eyed, gape-mouthed tourists in their own homeland, amazed and often overwhelmed by the unfamiliarity of the world around them.

There is little worse than waking up each day to a world that you feel less and less connected to, with new social rules spouting prolifically from new values that you do not understand or agree with, but that you must adhere to, or risk being ostracized. The reality is that if you *live too long* this will surely happen. The only option is to cut this party short. If you choose not to utilize that option, be forewarned—the autumn of your life has the potential for becoming frightfully lonely, disorientating, and demoralizing. Brace yourself.

About God

PART 1

For the sake of clarification, I must state the following. I will be referring to God in this essay as he or him. I do so to maintain coherence and readability. Please know that I am aware that a god-like being would not, could not, be contained in any form known to man and that whatever form, if any, he may possess, it certainly does not require reproductive organs—thereby canceling out any need for defending my reference to a particular gender identification.

Before I go on, let me make a few other things clear. I do not hold membership in that exclusive club of renowned philosophers who are best known for not agreeing on anything, except that they don't agree on anything. I do have vast experience working in the field of psychiatry, but I am not a psychologist or a psychiatrist. Then again, if I were either of these, I would be ashamed to admit it. There is little pride in being a condescending wannabe intellectual who chooses hoodwinking as a profession. Nor am I a theologian, a fancy title for a person who feels so uneasy with his faith that he must take up an occupation that allows him to search for some reassurance. I fear that many theologians eventually are forced to acknowledge the reality that the god they are searching for simply does not exist. Ironically, they are forced to face this unwelcome realization due to their own incessant research efforts. Do any of these guys find themselves one ancient text away from locking themselves in a hotel room with a bottle of Pappy Van Winkle, an eight ball of coke, and a couple of hookers, just before ending it all? I think . . . probably so. As for me, I am just an ordinary person. Admitting that I am no one special should make it clear that the following is not written for those who imagine themselves to be intellectuals. This is written for the common man by a common man who decided to do the uncommon by scrutinizing and questioning his given religion—something that he was taught from childhood to never do. This has led to some insights, which have led to some opinions, which I think are interesting and therefore worthy of sharing. I am, however, aware of that humbling truth—that one's assessment of one's own opinions is seldom accurate and often inflated. Having said that, all the following may turn out to be rubbish, something to throw out on that garbage heap of distorted perceptions and faulty conclusions. I will just have to leave the value of my offerings up to the discretion of the reader.

PART II

I began wondering how old the idea of a god could possibly be. The answer to that question turned out to be rather simple. First and foremost is that a god of any kind, as imagined by man, cannot be any older than man himself. Think about it. But to be much more exact, man's concept of a god can only be as old as man's ability to conceptualize abstract thought and to utilize advanced memory skills. Therefore, man's concept of a god can be no more than forty to seventy thousand years old, which is about the time that archaeological evidence indicates an advancement in the aforementioned mental prerequisites. As one would expect, this is the same timeframe in which evidence of a god image first appears. Before that there was no god, as far as humans were concerned. Anyone who would argue this point simply needs to reflect on the fact that for concepts to exist, such as a god, worship, and ritual, it requires a creature with an intellect that has evolved to a level of mental functioning that allowed for those abilities noted above. Without those abilities, cognition is concrete, limited, and focused on survival needs. Before he evolved to that required level, man simply did not have the mental wherewithal to conceive of a god, much less all the associated trappings.

Once mankind achieved that intellectual ability to conceptualize a god, he went wild. The history of polytheistic mythology demonstrates the reach of man's imagination and his gullibility. He simply believed in anything, which I guess is what one would expect from a mind that is in the early stages of its developmental process. Fears, generated by mysteries, were the driving force behind man's creation of supernatural beings. For millennia, he prayed and sacrificed to these figments of his imagination in some childlike hope that these abstracts could control things that he himself had no control over. As the human mind developed, problem-solving skills improved, and over time a few of the mysteries were unraveled. Once a mystery was solved, the god associated with that particular mystery was no longer needed and was simply discarded. This reflected the natural process of intellectual growth, eliminating the need for superstition. In addition, there was an improvement in organizational skills that came along with man's mental evolution. This ability, coupled with his more advanced problem-solving skills, made him receptive to consolidating the remaining mysteries and attributing them all to one provenance.

PART III

This leads us to the first recorded and clearly dated effort to institute monotheism, an effort attributed to Egyptian Pharaoh Akhenaten (reign 1353–1336 BCE). His attempt to make Aten (the sun god) the only god did not go over too well. He ticked off the priests, who supported the continuation of polytheism, but more importantly, he ticked off the people. The people of his kingdom were not ready for such a monumental change. They, along with the priests, assured that Akhenaten's concept of a single god died when he died.

One cannot mention monotheism without making a reference to Zoroastrianism. Its roots may very well go back as far or farther than 2000 BCE, but it was not firmly established in written history until the fifth century BCE when it served as the state religion for the Persian Empires. Some claim that Zoroastrianism was the first established monotheistic faith, but that is a bit wishy-washy. It did support the concept of one supreme god (Ahura Mazda), but other, lesser gods continued to be recognized. Still, it served as an important step toward the permanent formation of true monotheism. It is obvious that this belief system had a profound influence on the development of other religions, particularly Judaism and, in turn, Christianity.

The religions that surround the concept of the Judeo-Christian god all endorse Judaism's claim that theirs was the first legitimate monotheistic faith. Dates of origination asserted are many, ranging from 2000 BCE to 600 BCE. Yeah, that's quite a span, and it is quite confusing, but that is to be expected when religious bias runs rampant in the world of biblical archaeology. After a bit of personal research, I discovered a few interesting things. The first is that, outside of the Torah, there is no evidence that Moses, the supposed author of the first five Hebrew scriptures, ever existed. There also is no evidence that the events, as they are described in the Torah, ever occurred. In all probability, the origination of the Jewish monotheistic belief system is based on a story that was written and re-written by many authors over centuries, resulting in a product of their collective imaginations. I could go on and on pointing out the glaring absence of evidence to support those old biblical tales. I could offer numerous examples of persons who boast of their scholastic status, offering up faulty logic to justify scriptural content and biblical claims that make no sense whatsoever. If I really wanted to punish myself and the reader, I could provide limitless examples of the embarrassing efforts of the faithful, blinded by their desperate need to believe, endlessly trying to make square pegs fit into round holes. But regurgitating such information seems like a waste of time and words when anyone can review such for themselves with a few simple stokes on the computer keyboard or can witness such for themselves by making a quick visit to a local synagogue, neighborhood church, or evangelical superdome.

Another point of interest that seems obvious is that the religious beliefs of the Jewish people were rooted in polytheism and for hundreds of years remained polytheistic. The concept of monotheism was not a sudden awakening or an overnight transformation with a clearly identifiable start date. The idea was tossed around, repeatedly sputtered out when tried, and only caught a foothold after a very slow adaptation process. It is very likely that the concept of the Jewish god and the entire belief system connected to it was borrowed from other cultures, like a collage that was arranged and rearranged till it suited the purpose of the upper echelon of Jewish religious leaders of that day. The Jewish god (Yahweh) is probably a reflection of

Zoroastrianism's supreme god (Ahura Mazda), and the core concepts of Judaism probably originated from this same ancient religion or from a variety of others.

That said, the first *successful* effort to establish a purely monotheistic religion can, I think, be justifiably claimed by the Jewish people. It is impossible to give a definite date of their final transition to monotheism, so I'm going to go with 600 BCE—give or take a hundred years. That would be around the time that the first full draft of the Torah is believed to have been completed. That is probably just as good a guess as any.

Some religions do not see the value of having a personal and unique god-like figure. Rather, they value the expedience of simply stealing one. Such is the case with Christianity. By the first century, the masses were hungry for a new religious movement. There were numerous prophets wandering about selling their religious wares: some were charlatans, some madmen, and some sincere altruists, obsessed with their personal mythos. It is interesting to note here that madmen and altruists are difficult to distinguish when observing only their external appearance and behaviors. The difference is that the delusions of madmen tend to go in circles, are less organized, and never come to any definite resolution. The delusions of an altruist, however, are organized, having defined goals and a clear direction that gently lead you into their world of fantasy, which is often indistinguishable from pathological psychosis. Both are creatures who are barely hanging on, with a sweaty grip, to the rim of reality.

Anyway, as I was saying before I wandered off, there were many belief options floating around back then that had the potential for becoming the next big thing. It was only by a freak accident, when particular events collided at a particular time in a particularly fertile place, that Christianity was born as the unwanted and often unacknowledged offspring of Judaism. Whereas Judaism had borrowed its concept of god from other cultures and then developed it to fit its needs, Christianity saved itself the trouble and simply kidnapped the Jewish god and made him their own. It was a simple maneuver that involved producing a character that fit, or was made to fit, the messianic prophecies sprinkled throughout the Hebrew Bible. Once that messiah was produced, the Christian religion was directly connected to the very heart of Judaism, giving it a right to claim the Jewish god as its own. This religion started out low-key, recruiting the meek and the humble, who were willing to turn the other cheek, but it soon showed its true colors.

Christianity, a monster like the Hydra of Greek mythology, has been hanging around for the past two thousand years, refusing to die, sprouting two denominations for every one that failed, and constantly spitting its missionary venom, thereby poisoning the four corners of the earth. It concealed itself behind a facade of love, peace, mercy, and forgiveness in order to gain access into the hearts and minds of the innocent who, once taken in, were brainwashed and then used as agents of hatred, war, bigotry, and genocide. The atrocities committed by

"Christians" have been so heinous, it would stretch the bounds of decency to describe. The fact that this religion has survived for two thousand years and continues causing mayhem is a sad but eye-opening acknowledgment of the very slow pace of man's intellectual evolution and confirms the fact that he is still just a child—a very bad child.

PART IV

It is estimated that we humans and our ancestors have been here on earth for six million years. But, as mentioned earlier, man has only possessed the ability to conceptualize a god for forty to seventy thousand years. So, doing the math, it seems as if a god has been absent during the entire six million years except for this nanosecond that we are now experiencing. The best that mankind has been able to come up with so far is a god that is an idyllic version of himself, one that he uses to glorify his few good qualities and excuse his many shortcomings. Man presents his imagined god in such a fantastical manner that it is hard to believe that such a god exists or has ever existed.

I personally believe that a single entity that we'll call "God" (with a capital G) is real. But I think that entity is far beyond the reach of man's feeble imagination. It would be impossible for us to determine his origin or even prove his existence. And we can never figure out, using our concept of earth time, how long he has been around. To my knowledge, eternity (having no beginning and no end) is not measurable. Many say that there is much to indicate that God exists, but no one has provided any factual evidence. Then again, wouldn't it be surprising to find evidence of God in this reality since God is not of this reality? The earth and everything in it may arguably be a product of God, through which his essence may very well flow. But that is not the same as verifiable evidence of his existence, and it certainly has nothing to do with identifying his origin or understanding the reality that God exists in. It is very much like admiring the most magnificent examples of art that you can possibly imagine, all of which have been created by unknown artists. You can experience such awe-inspiring art through most, if not all, of your sensory organs, and you can even appreciate some art on an intellectual level. But even amid that sensorial excitement and intellectual arousal, it is the creation that you are experiencing. That experience, no matter how joyous, does not provide proof of its creator's origin or even of the existence of any one particular creator. The art may have been produced by several creators working together, or a pallet of paints, tipped over by an earthquake, may have fallen on a piece of canvas, creating, by chance, something beautiful. Perhaps the art was created by an advanced form of artificial intelligence—in which case we would be searching for the creator of the creator. The creation, the art, only suggests that at some point there may have been a creator or creators, or that some event occurred that produced the creation. All else is speculation. It is outside of our intellectual capacity to accurately conceive of that unknown artist. There simply is no knowledge base to work from.

Does anyone really believe that man has the required mental or sensory faculties to conceptualize God, much less understand him or the reality that he exists in? Isn't it obvious that man simply does not possess the ability to comprehend a god who creates and maintains not only the insignificant planet of Earth but also 21.6 sextillion other planets (inhabited or not), one septillion or more stars, and billions of galaxies in the known universe, not to mention the likelihood of other unknown universes? Mankind trying to understand the true reality of God is like a sloth trying to break into a Brinks truck. Even with the key, it is a near impossibility; without the key, there is no chance at all. The key to understanding God is to achieve a god-like intelligence. I had to laugh a little as I wrote these words because I know that there have been and are human beings who, in some state of outrageous egotism, believe themselves to have achieved some god-like status. If you ever begin to feel that way about yourself, just remember that you are the sloth—without the key.

PART V

We must accept that our concept of God, in any shape or form, is but a figment of our limited imaginations, or maybe something worse. In the Christian world, many people believe that man was made in God's image. When they think of God, they think of themselves. To me that has always seemed like self-worship or some attempt to place ourselves on God's level. As for myself, I have always thought of God as being something totally foreign in appearance and composition to anything human. If you believe in the omnipresence of God, you are likely to agree with me. This quality of being continuously and simultaneously present throughout the whole of creation eliminates any possibility of God possessing a physical form, at least not one that we can conceive. It certainly eliminates any possibility that he resembles any of his creatures—man included. I doubt if he has an *appearance* at all. I think he may be a consciousness but one without borders, one that reaches far beyond the capacity of petty modern technology and the finite abilities of man's comprehension. I think he is as large or larger than the universe. Having no fixed form, he can adapt, spread out, and fill in all available space. He disseminates by way of innumerable appendages in lengths adequate to reach into every corner of every galaxy. Those appendages are sophisticated, highly specialized sensory organs, constantly collecting limitless, detailed data from sources and places that man cannot envision. They gradually decrease from being galactic in size to less than microscopic so that God can enter every possible crevice and pour through every capillary of creation. God is therefore present in all things because he is infused into all things. At some molecular level, all things, including man, are part of God rather than separate from God. This suggests to me that mankind is the equivalent of a submicroscopic tip at the periphery of one of these extremities. This thought always silences that loud-talking braggart who lives in my head (ego). It, too, pulls the rug out from under the lie of mankind's importance and reveals the truth of our insignificance. I love my personal concept of God, but I must admit that it is just a guess created by my imagination. It is likely a guess that is just as wrong as everyone else's guesses. It would probably be best if we all just stopped trying to conceptualize God. To even try displays our arrogance and reveals our ignorance of the limits of our own mental capacities. Our best efforts tend to be embarrassingly elementary, and our worst efforts anthropomorphic and disrespectful.

If you believe in God, you must accept that you believe in something for which there is no factual evidence. If you believe—then just believe. You must allow yourself to be comfortable knowing that your faith is rooted in emotion, something absolutely foreign to your intellect. To find that comfort you must acknowledge that there is no need for rationalizing, justifying, or verifying. Your private and personal feelings, which you do not impose on other folks, are your own and do not require any defense. If you feel or sense the presence of God, be joyous and be satisfied. Let go of trying to understand or even trying to imagine God. The chasm between our intellect and the required intellect is simply too vast to ever cross.

PART VI

I take heart in knowing that God makes himself known to us through certain celestial connections that allow for communication, without the corruption and static of intellectual inquiry. I know it is in silence that his voice is most pronounced. I have found that it helps to find a place of solitude far away from the interference of man-made things and as close as possible to those remnants of God's original creation. That place is Nature, where his quintessence is still present and a reflection of his unimaginable power can be seen. I refer to these communications as memorable phenomena: those rare times when I am freed from the prison of my human form. In those moments, I am in a semi-conscious state, barely tethered to my accustomed level of consciousness, carried off into a vast emptiness by a sense of peacefulness that is so exquisite I almost stop breathing, as if I do not need air. There is a boundless jubilation that is generated from a sense of floating then falling, over and over, as I adjust to the weightlessness of my transcendental self. A tingling runs through me that builds into a sensation like an adrenaline storm that forces me to open myself up and allow everything around me to become part of me and me part of it. I travel in a space void of time, experiencing a hypnotic serenity that inundates my mind and produces a profound sense of security. There I am blissfully unaware and well protected from the evils that prowl the earth. Absent, too, is that childish hope that contentment will be found during my mortal existence. On the rarest of occasions, I am carried back, back beyond memory; back through my subconscious to the far side of my unconscious; back before I was a blastocyst implanted in the wall of my mother's uterus, or even before fertilization; back to the point of my origination, where the only part of me that existed was an atman. There, in a blissful abyss, I am surrounded by trillions of my fellow companions, all travelers on an eternal journey. We patiently and happily wait (sometimes for thousands or even millions of years) to peek through that occasional sliver of light that breaks through the veil, revealing a different view, a different perception, a different reality of eternity. It is not my scheduled moment of departure from mortal life, so I am gently awakened to face the remainder of my human existence. Having had a glimpse of what awaits, I return rejuvenated and fortified to forge ahead through that messy collection of human affairs and earthly events that constitute life. All is bearable knowing that I will be rewarded for my struggles with one grand prize—escape.

After reading the above, you may be thinking, "Wow, that sounded bizarre, akin to some old hippie's recollection of an LSD trip." I can assure you that the experiences described are not drug induced, but they may involve something similar to psychotic episodes. I say this because any contact with God's reality or even an acceptance of God's existence requires a psychotic break of sorts. All religious faith is based on the belief in an alternate reality where God resides and where our Elysium awaits. To step into, or up to, that alternate reality requires a letting go of the short-term, insignificant existence that we presently find ourselves in. Memorable phenomena, such as I have described, only seem odd because we are captured in this small pocket of air that circles our little planet. We are blind and ignorant to the magnitude of creation. I think we may have allowed ourselves to be taken in by science. Its reassurances that "final answers" to the important questions have been found may have squelched our curiosity and anesthetized our imagination. Too, we have become dependent on modern technology and addicted to the crippling convenience that it provides. I fear it has become what Karl Marx once called religion—"the opium of the masses." Curiosity and imagination, coupled with initiative, are the tools that allow us to dig into and through this consciousness to discover what may be beyond. Without those tools we are corralled in this single reality.

CONCLUSION

Our perception of actuality is based on the senses that we employ to collect various types of data. The type and degree of data collected is solely dependent upon the capacity of those senses. Experiencing another reality may just be a matter of activating a sense that we already possess but that few of us are aware of. Awakening that "sixth sense" (for lack of a better term) may be simpler than one might think. First, we must shake free of those blinders, those *final answers*, which science has strapped to the sides of our heads. They obscure our vision to what is all around us, allowing only a narrow view, focusing on but a small bit of what is and what is possible. Second, we must sever our love affair with technology. Only then will we be able to throw off that mental slothfulness that stifles our spirit of inquiry and suffocates our creative thoughts. Once relieved of such encumbrances, our minds are free to experience God in our own unique ways. That experience may or may not be like the description I have shared of my own spiritual journey. I am sure God has many methods of communication. But however he chooses to speak to us, I believe that his message is always similar. He wishes for us to be at peace with the fact that he exists. He reveals to us that this peace cannot be gained by intellectual exertion but rather is found in the center of one's being as a confident, unwavering, emotional commitment.

On the topic of living a life that assures we remain in his good graces, he offers one warning, a little advice and something to contemplate. He warns us to be wary of religious leaders or spiritual guides, especially those who advocate reliance on any book of instruction. They are liars who encourage others to believe in texts they claim are sacred scripture but are known to have been written by unholy hands. He, instead, encourages us to reflect on the fact that if we believe in him, no guide is needed; we already know the way. He advises us to embrace our short period of corporeality. Enjoy the experiences that it has to offer. Place all adversity in its proper place by remembering that this existence lasts less time than it takes a falling star to travel across the night sky. And he leaves us with a snippet of knowledge that provides a comforting reassurance. Earthly reality is not separate and apart from eternity. It is a continuation of eternity. Try to think of the various types and levels of consciousness that might flash past during an endless metaphysical journey. In this scenario, we are passengers on a mystical train looking out of our windows. The perceptions that we experience change, but the fact that we are continuously traveling through eternity does not change. When we leave this life, this reality, there is nothing to fear. It is no more than turning our heads away from the window and finding great relief in the realization that we have never left the train.

Adrift

The recognition and acceptance of the human condition as it relates to intrinsic aloneness is an interesting concept for discussion and one that challenges the imagination. But, in reality, forced and relentless aloneness is an extremely dire situation. Finding yourself stuck in such a state can be likened to finding yourself clinging to a piece of driftwood in the middle of an ocean. Panic will surely set in if there is a lack of fortitude.

Even if that panic is managed, you will eventually be forced to surrender to the overwhelming enormity of the emptiness that surrounds you. You are only saved from slipping under the surface by the currents that routinely deliver other survivors to your immediate vicinity. The sighting of another causes a revitalization of energy that you thought was exhausted. It is manifested in a frenzied effort to reach out and make contact with the other. That desperate effort is motivated by a need to bond through touch, language, and shared experiences. The reciprocal appreciation for each other's presence acts as a life preserver for you and for the other, keeping you both from sinking into the depths of despair.

But even during these life-sustaining connections, the motion of the ocean and the pull of the current is constantly testing and trying your efforts to hold on to the other. Still, it is only through these tenuous and frequently temporary interrelations that you are able to find moments of reprieve from that aloneness, which is constantly trying to swallow you up. The presence of the other offers no hope of escape from your circumstances of oneness. Rather it provides a reassurance, a confirmation, of your existence that can only be provided, it seems, by the existence of another.

This need for reassurance, which haunts each one of us, is rooted in a skepticism related to the validity of our perceived existence. Most often we can shrug off or fend off that skepticism, but occasionally it forces its way into our thoughts. This doubt manifests itself in questions. Did we exist before this life, before this reality? If we did, does that mean that this is just one of a sequence of realities? If so, why isn't there some evidence of our previous realities? There is no reason we would keep them secret from ourselves. And if there was nothing before this reality, doesn't that suggest at the end of this reality there is nothing more? That dredges up the age-old question of does God really exist, or did man create God to ease his fear of the nothingness that awaits him? And finally, we must ask, are we experiencing true reality or is this all just the product of a mishap in human evolution? Has that mishap left human beings afflicted with an unharnessed imagination that distorts the perception we have of ourselves and our world? If our consciousness is unreliable, then isn't it possible that we are not *who* or even *what* we think we are?

All this doubt about our own existence is placed at ease simply by another person sharing a few thoughts and experiences that we can relate to. The mere presence of another assures us that even if we are not who or what we think we are, and even if we are existing in some distorted reality, at least we are not alone. Such reassurance calms our minds, preventing them from venturing too far by questioning too much. Luckily our fear of the truth draws a line in the sand. It warns us not to approach the one query that sits precariously on a cliff ledge that drops off into madness. It protects us from asking the question: "Are those other people who reassure us of our existence real or just creations of a distorted consciousness?" The answer to that question has the potential to push us over the edge.

Save the Planet; Stop Making Those Babies

PART 1

The first law of thermodynamics confirms that energy cannot be destroyed or created. So, it is fair to say that there is only so much energy on our planet and within the confines of its immediate atmosphere. Let's say that we (human beings) are containers for the energy that is required to maintain our metabolism and the basic biological functions of our physical beings. Let's say that each human being equals one hundred units of energy. In addition, let's say that the environmental cost of maintaining each individual for an average life span is equivalent to the very low guesstimate of ten thousand units of energy. There are approximately 7.9 billion human beings, so that would come to 7.9 quadrillion units of energy captured or being utilized by human beings and therefore not available for other purposes. Is it possible that this amount of energy subtracted from the total quantity is enough to cause major decreases in biodiversity, the disappearance of natural resources, and changes in atmospheric conditions? Can all these issues be the natural consequences of an increased human population monopolizing an excess of the available energy? Perhaps human behavior is a secondary cause of environmental destruction rather than the primary cause as is commonly believed. Perhaps the simple fact that too many humans exist is causing an unsustainable imbalance. It is very possible that every human being born, in excess of what is necessary to maintain the species, takes us one step closer to planetary destruction. Is the answer to solving many of the world's major problems just a matter of asking people to stop reproducing? And if that is so, do we possess the restraint necessary to stop ourselves? I think—probably not.

I say probably not because we are still driven by a primitive instinct to procreate. That simple, basic instinct rooted in our very DNA was hardwired into us at the earliest stages of man's evolution. That drive to reproduce was designed with a switch that once turned on was not meant to be turned off, and for good reason. In the beginning, human beings, like all other species, were simply struggling to survive. That meant they had to reproduce at a rate that would maintain numbers sufficient to assure long-term viability. Early on, humans had a tough time keeping those numbers up. Around 130,000 years ago, there may have been as few as 200,000 or 300,000 humans in existence. With such low numbers, just one or two natural disasters, on any major scale, could have easily pushed mankind into extinction. For example, the super volcano Toba, which erupted around 70,000 BCE, blew 650 miles of vaporized rock into the air, causing catastrophic environmental effects worldwide. As a result, it is possible that the entire population of human beings was reduced to roughly a few thousand reproductive adults. Other factors that made it hard for early man to keep his head above water included extreme climate changes as well as the unimaginable number of stronger, faster predators who thought of humans as snack food. Of course, man also played the role of predator. But in playing that role, he actually increased his risk of not surviving. After all, trying to bring down mammoths with a pointy stick was a high-risk business that often resulted in fatal injuries.

PART II

The exact life expectancy of folks way back then is hard to guess since there is not much in the way of solid evidence available. But I think we can be sure no one had to worry about retirement planning. To get at least some idea of how fragile life was during *prehistoric* times, we are forced to reference records and archaeological findings from our earliest *historical* times. That data indicates that during the development of early civilization, one in every four births ended in death within the first year of life. Approximately 50 percent never made it through childhood. Remember that these infant and childhood mortality rates are reflective of early civilization. The folks who existed in this early *historical* period were living in high cotton compared to their *prehistoric* ancestors, who did not enjoy the benefits of advanced social structure with its agrarian lifestyle but rather struggled along in an unstructured, unpredictable, unforgiving environment. It is therefore easy to imagine that the prospects for childhood survival were even bleaker during those times long before civilization. As for the life expectancy of those lucky few who reached adulthood, it wasn't much rosier. The great majority of anthropologists agree that if an early prehistoric man lived beyond thirty years old, he would be considered a senior citizen.

I think all the above makes it pretty clear why that relentless drive to reproduce was necessary if early man was to have any hope of surviving as a species. From the time that hormones jumpstarted his virility until the day he died, the human male's primary focus, and in fact his entire purpose for existence, was to copulate to procreate. He was motivated to perform only by the force of his instinct, and that instinct was totally free to express itself. He was not concerned about pleasing his mate physically or emotionally. He was not preoccupied with getting a job, striving for promotions, work schedules, or vacation plans. He was not bothered by having to be socially appropriate, showing concern for other people's feelings, or complying with all the other aspects of that stifling creation of mankind yet to be invented—morality. He was not even worried about the welfare of his own offspring since he did not possess the ability to conceptualize parental responsibility. In fact, he did not even possess the intellectual capacity to understand that they were *his* offspring. Young ones may have had some value as bait to draw something in that the group hoped to overpower and feast on for a few days. And they could have come in handy if a predator was hot on the heels of an adult male. Tossing a toddler over his shoulder would have served as the perfect distraction, providing those extra few seconds the adult male needed to escape. And it was imperative that he did escape so he could assure the survival of the species by continuing to copulate. He did have one concern, though it was somewhat superficial, and that was his desire to hold on to any females in his possession. They were, after all, the least dangerous and the most pleasant method of relieving that worrisome sexual tension. So yes, he was motivated to defend them if the risk to his personal existence was not too great.

PART III

Early man did not know why he was obsessed with that overwhelming desire to copulate. He just knew that he was plagued with a queasy feeling that originated in his gonads and ignited a compulsion that drove him to sexually penetrate anything that would hold still for just one, maybe two, minutes. Yes, he preferred a fertile female of his own species, but in desperate times a close cousin that wandered too far from her simian tribe, a friendly Neanderthal or Denisovan with a wandering eye, or a goat with a tolerant disposition would do the trick. If all else failed, manual stimulation or simply lying prostrate and rocking on an erection would work. Anything to create enough friction to release that damned endless supply of human seed. Left to collect, it resulted in an aching, like catching a half-assed kick to the scrotum—not enough to double you over but just enough to irritate the shit out of you. When not relieved, that irritation would manifest itself in unnecessary risk taking, excessive assertiveness, and random, unprovoked aggression. It could involve physical abuse of weaker members of the group, displays of physical prowess, and physical challenges that often resulted in life-or-death struggles for dominance.

When civilization appeared, it stifled the release of that sexual tension by creating behavioral expectations, moral considerations, judicial consequences, courting rituals, and marital contracts. This social circus forced males to jump through every kind of hoop imaginable just to get a nut. The process was unbearable, so ways were found to get around it. A love–hate relationship with prostitution was created, which persists today. Society also incorporated a universal forgiveness for male promiscuity into its already confusing concept of morality. Unfortunately, we failed to be so benevolent toward the females who fell prey to these licentious males. I guess someone had to take the blame since some pious charlatans posing as holy men had decided sex was a sin. Females turned out to be the perfect scapegoats, having little voice and no clout. The Bible, having established a history of them being the seducers of men since the Garden of Eden, was used to seal their fate. But still, there was an excess of male sexual tension that had to go somewhere, and it did. It very well may be the reason that human beings became such a violent species. Man's history is marred with wars that have slaughtered and abused billions. Wars could be viewed as random explosions of that barely contained frustration man carries around inside himself. It is always looking for an excuse to vent. War has always been the perfect outlet, giving license to murder, rape, and pillage.

Younger males reading this will find certain portions of it extremely familiar. Older, seasoned males will find all of it familiar. Well, maybe except for that comment related to bestiality. Hopefully, most guys today are in possession of some sort of standards that will restrain them from becoming sexually involved with a goat or other barnyard animals. But that aside, males with some life experience under their belts will totally understand all I have described, from that queasy feeling in the gonads to that need for the extremes of violence. Why is that? Why would any modern male understand something that originated in the very beginnings of man's evolution and is rooted in the most primitive aspects of his being? Well, because that very same relentless drive to copulate, to procreate, which originated in our very earliest ancestors, has not changed over hundreds of thousands, possibly millions, of years—not one bit. But other things have changed.

PART IV

Whether by design or by accident, the human brain increased in size and complexity. But the most important development was cortical folding, which allowed the cerebral cortex, the thin outer layer of neurons and its associated projections, to attain a large surface area relative to brain volume. Over time, man reached a certain intellectual level, which resulted in an advanced knowledge base. That knowledge base allowed for reductions in the infant and childhood mortality rates and increased the global life expectancy. As mentioned earlier, the infant mortality rate during prehistoric times was at least 25 percent, and the childhood mortality rate is estimated to have been 50 percent or greater. Today, the infant mortality rate is 2.9 percent, and the childhood mortality rate averages around 4.6 percent. The average life expectancy of prehistoric man is thought to have been thirty years. The global average life expectancy for 2020 was 72.8 years. The earth is now home to approximately 7.9 billion human beings compared to the few hundred thousand of early prehistoric times. Obviously, the original purpose of the survival instinct as it relates to procreation has been more than successful. So much so that continued propagation threatens the planet's ability to support this ever-expanding super surplus of human beings. The tremendous changes in mortality rates and the astonishing increase in the number of human beings has only been possible because our meddlesome intellect has successfully disrupted many of Nature's most effective culling methods. That has left the proliferation of mankind unchecked. The uncontrolled expansion of a population is never good for any species, and it has not been good for human beings. Man is racing toward his own destruction. While doing so, he has caused and continues to cause massive collateral damage to his fellow creatures and to the earth itself.

So that brings us to this realization: We are equipped with the same drive to survive now, in the twenty-first century, that we were originally equipped with when man first appeared on earth. There have been no updates, even though an update is certainly in order. Mother Nature equipped man, in those earliest of days, to meet the demands of his circumstances and the challenges of a harsh environment. A sexual drive that once switched on could not be switched off made sense for a creature who was not meant to live more than thirty years, especially when you consider that he was struggling to maintain the viability of his species while faced with extreme rates of infant and childhood mortality. And this was made even more difficult since he didn't reach puberty until his twelfth, maybe as late as his fifteenth, year. So, in total, he was only given around fifteen years of sexual maturity to do his part to assure that the human species survived. This was asking a lot, but Mother Nature knew that if man just kept on humping (pun intended) he would make it. One could say that she (Mother Nature) had a formula that took into consideration the hardships presented by the prehistoric environment and how those hardships negatively affected mortality rates. This she weighed against the male's determination to copulate and his potential effectiveness related to reproduction. As is common in nature, such formulas are based on very precise calculations. The formula allowed for mankind to have a good chance to survive but kept the numbers limited so they did not threaten their own or other species by exhausting available resources. Mother Nature did not anticipate that evolution would make a few tweaks to the human brain, tweaks that would result in a problematic intellect. She could not have predicted that this intellect would disturb the very precise calculation that was keeping everything in balance.

PART V

That irritating, overwhelming demand to procreate persists even though it has lost its purpose. It has become the very bane of every grown man's existence. Yes, it has its appeal early on in a young man's life, but it soon becomes an annoying diversion, distracting us from completing the necessary tasks of modern life. Imagine how much time is wasted by the typical male who spends most of his waking hours trying to penetrate somebody or thinking about penetrating somebody when he should be focused on advancing his education, getting ahead on the job, securing his finances, or working to maintain the integrity of his marriage vow? Once copulation for the purpose of procreation was the ultimate creative act, one that the very survival of mankind depended on. In today's world, it has become a source of vast destruction. How many relationships have been ruined by that obsession with coitus, which has the power to drag even the unwilling into infidelity? Even those at the pinnacle of our social hierarchy, who have it all, are not immune. I doubt a week goes by without a report of another CEO, politician, or priest sacrificing everything for the sake of an illicit and seedy affair. How many children find themselves in single-parent or foster homes because some irresponsible male, unwilling or unable to control his urges, has unprotected sex with some gullible female, even though he has no intention of being responsible for the consequences of his actions?

We have convinced ourselves that the three pounds of neurons and synapses confined in our skullcaps make us superior to all other species. So, isn't it about time that we call on that superior mental capacity to get a handle on all this excessive copulating and solve this problem of overpopulation? We do love to brag about the power of our intellect, but that supposed intellectual prowess has proven itself impotent when trying to control our base instincts. The male's desire to copulate is still easily tempted beyond all intellectual restraint by any female willing to don a French maid's costume and a pair of fishnet stockings. The power of the male sexual drive is evidenced by the fact that most males are sexual predators by nature—not criminal predators, but sexual predators, nevertheless. As predators, they search out consensual opportunities with the insecure, the gullible, the emotionally damaged, and those without the worldliness necessary to avoid their tricks and traps. Most men, at one point or another, fit into this predatory category. It is only in the presence of the very oldest males that a woman can let her guard down without fear of a sexual advance. This is not because older men are free of their need to procreate or that they are free from their obsession with coitus, but rather because they have lost the charms necessary to persuade a potential mate or have possibly lost their physical ability to perform.

We would hope that the more intellectual members of our species (females) might save us by simply refusing to be impregnated. But only recently have some women been able to stifle their own instinct to reproduce by opening their eyes to the numerous life choices available to them other than motherhood. Unfortunately, many, too many, are still under the spell of their traditional indoctrination, with its propaganda that falsely claims true womanhood can only be achieved through motherhood.

CONCLUSION

I am afraid that all of this suggests we will continue to expand the numbers of our population exponentially. We could be saved if our brain was to evolve quickly enough, thereby becoming strong enough, to overpower our desire to breed. But the reality is that evolution cannot be hurried and moves at a tedious pace, so there is little hope for us there. Perhaps our intellectual elite will come together and harness the collective power of their minds to tackle the task of finding a solution. But even if we accept that we are only a few copulations away from world destruction, would we be receptive to a scientifically proven method of controlling our sexual drive? Would we all be willing to do or not do whatever we have to do in order to survive as a species? Is that really possible? When I consider our very poor history of getting along with our fellow man and our total inability to cooperate when faced with recent global disaster issues (e.g., COVID), I think—probably not. I fear that the instinct that once assured our survival will very likely be the thing that assures our doom.

Terra

How you have fallen from heaven,
O star of the morning, son of the dawn!
You have been cut down to the earth . . .
Isaiah 14:12

Imagine you are a soul, a tiny seed of consciousness, a speck or two of morality wrapped in a spark of celestial energy flying through the infinite vastness of eternity. You are as content as can be. Then, veering off course, ever so slightly, you suddenly find yourself caught in the gravitational pull of the planet Terra, located within the Orionem Brachium of the Lactea Via Galaxy. This planet possesses an infamous reputation. It is known for having a seductive appearance from a distance, which conceals a wickedness which reigns below. It is rumored that Terra is where that ungrateful and overly ambitious entity known as Lucifer was exiled after his fall from God's good grace. It is there, on Terra, that Lucifer's offspring are said to dwell. It is a place to be avoided. But now, due to a minor navigational mishap, your fate, like the sinister gravitational pull of this planet, is inescapable.

You are dragged to the planet's surface and through a dark portal, then sealed deep within a fertilized ovum. That ovum evolves into a parasitic cell called a zygote, which becomes a blastocyst. The blastocyst then transmutes into an embryo, which then grows into something called a fetus. This free-loading fetus continues to grow, overstaying its welcome until it is eventually rejected and ejected from its host. You, that small spark of celestial energy, imprisoned in that fetus, find yourself delivered into a hellish world of violence and emotional turmoil. The fetus, more properly referred to as an infant once separated from its host, continues to transform itself until it becomes a mature offspring of Lucifer.

Lucifer creates these creatures (his children) through a whimsical use of simian DNA, which results in what is called *Homo sapiens* (a.k.a. humans). A single soul's presence in each of these humans is essential to their existence. Each siphons off the energy from a soul's celestial spark, utilizing it to ignite and then maintain their life force. Lucifer's goal in producing these cretins is quantity versus quality, so they turn out to be inferior, simpleminded anthropoids, with a low intellectual ceiling and brutish behaviors. They are a disgusting life form, with the male of the species dominated by an unrelenting sexual impulse that forces it to release its seed anywhere and everywhere. The preferred method for the release of their erotic desires is through the conquest of females, of any age, but particularly those of child-bearing years. Females are usually won over by various types of trickery. But if that fails, the males are not beyond violently forcing the issue. These are self-absorbed organisms, consumed by greed and driven by their gluttonous compulsions. They are walking, talking sewage-filtration machines that are constantly converting their overindulgence into foul waste, which necessitates frequent elimination to minimize any interruption to their voracious consumption.

Of all the complex life forms, in all the universes, humans possess the least intelligence. Simple, gullible, and blinded to their own limited cognition, they easily talk themselves into believing that they are "highly evolved." They are like great baboons, strutting about loudly boasting of the great progress they have made in solving problems. But the truth is that they create two problems for every one they solve, and their limited ability to learn from experience condemns them to a perpetual nightmare of endlessly solving problems of their own making.

They are a collection of cheap, fragile bits and pieces of common elements fabricated, in a slipshod manner, into an embarrassing example of anatomy. They are a rickety race, made up of a little oxygen, carbon, hydrogen, nitrogen, calcium, and phosphorus, with trace amounts of potassium, sulfur, sodium, chlorine, and magnesium thrown in to hold the whole mess together. Like most items of mass production, they are intended to last for only a short time and to serve only one purpose. In this case, that purpose is to fulfill their master's desires.

It must be understood that Lucifer is not of the physical world, so he needs human physiology to connect himself to all the sensuality of human reality. In other words, humans act as instruments through which Lucifer can experience and enjoy all the grotesque sins that his deranged consciousness conceives. He instills in these beings an ultra-susceptibility to temptation and a hyper-proclivity to commit evil. To encourage the most horrific sins only requires Lucifer whispering in their ears that they are special, assuring them that they are the children of God, that they can be forgiven for any sin—therefore, they can commit any sin. To allow himself to fully experience the exquisite turmoil of human existence, Lucifer provides his children with an array of emotions such as love, hate, joy, anger, guilt, happiness, envy, and melancholy. He provides these, the basic components necessary to play the sadomasochistic game referred to as human life, knowing full well that these emotions are far too complicated and far too powerful to be managed by humans. But still, he allows them to experience these emotions as a way of tormenting them so that through their emotional exhilaration and anguish he can achieve voyeuristic pleasure.

And so there you are, a celestial force, a soul, imprisoned in one of these human containers that exists in a world of endless sin and constant pandemonium. In time you realize that you are not alone. Each day, three to four hundred thousand souls are captured by the gravitational pull of this diabolical planet and imprisoned in these containers. You pray for them and for yourself. You long for the demise of your container and constantly dream of regaining your full celestial power, which is your only hope of returning to your home in eternity. God hears your prayers and sends divine support, not to help you survive in this world but rather to help you escape this world. Angelic forces, licensed by God to use any means necessary, constantly rain down destruction on these humans in an effort to rescue as many souls as possible. God devises and oversees droughts, starvation, diseases, accidents, murders, suicides, wars, genocides, and natural disasters that destroy one hundred and fifty to two hundred thousand of these vile creatures per day. But these children of Lucifer are in a constant rut. They multiply on the surface of Terra as rapidly as germs multiply on a rotting carcass, and so the hijacking of souls, through the theft of their celestial energies, continues. This battle, with no foreseeable end, is the result of the unimaginable: an apparent fault in God's judgment. God's mercy allows for Lucifer's continued existence, and due to that continued existence, millions of souls have and will suffer the horrors of hell—the terror of Terra. No one is in a position to question God, but still, it is hard not to wonder.

Finally, unexpectedly, after decades of pleading, your individual horror story ends abruptly with the termination of your container. Simply by luck, the human that you are imprisoned in is crushed under a fallen tree. That tree is blown down by a wind produced by the wings of a seraph who just happened to be passing by. Suddenly you are free! For a moment you are stunned by the reality of your freedom, but then you rocket into the atmosphere, then beyond to outer space, then, using every bit of your celestial power to reach supersonic speed, you break through the veil that borders eternity. You only allow yourself to slow down to a comfortable cruise when you know that you are beyond any possible reach of the Lactea Via Galaxy. The joy of being back to infinity is almost limitless, but something is just slightly different. The joy of eternal existence is somehow diminished by having experienced life on Terra. The memory of pre-life innocence has been tarnished and post-life existence is stained with the knowledge of sin in its most depraved forms. You fear that the total peace you knew before Terra will be forever out of reach. You can only hope that, after a mega-annum or two, you may be able to put the memory of having been in hell out of your immediate consciousness. For the time being, a little extra attention is given to your location and your course—just to be sure no navigational errors occur. A little vigilance seems appropriate now that you know *that you never know* when the devil may reach out and grab you.

The Lie

Just as we all share the same first sin (a lie), we also all share the same motivation for committing that sin, and the facilitators of that first sin always share the same names.

PART 1

The first time we lie, we split ourselves in two. Before that lie, we are an innocent, singular being living within our human shell, ignorant of sin, and due to that ignorance, incapable of committing sin. We are simple creatures driven by simple desires that are all related to an uncomplicated instinct to survive. This is our natural self, our real self, our Original Self. This self will always be the most intimate part of us, but its human shell is about to get crowded because here comes company. A seemingly minor event, our first lie, changes everything. It begins with a bang, bang, banging on the door that disturbs the Original Self and awakens a Second Self. At the door is an aggressive salesperson with a predatory air and the hypnotic stare normally associated with a viper. He is determined to sell the idea that lying is not only okay but is a necessary skill for the evolved and modern human being. He knows that the Original Self is far beyond his powers of persuasion, so he focuses his sales pitch on that Second Self, which he has just awoken. His wares are books of knowledge. Their titles are: *The Book of Right and Wrong* and *The Book of Good and Evil.* He admits that these are both created by man and not by some supernatural being, as is often claimed. He forthrightly declares that the content of these books is geared toward preparing one to become proficient in the lie, in deception, in illusion—in the old thimblerig, if you will. He explains that the given definitions of the terms right and wrong, good and evil, have permeable edges. For example, a good act can be committed for the wrong reasons, and evil can be committed for the right reasons. The rights of yesterday can and most often do become the wrongs of today. The wrongs of today can become the rights of tomorrow. In addition, the determination of good or evil and right or wrong has to do with the time period we live in, the culture we happen to be born in, and the religious, nationalistic, and political beliefs that we choose or find ourselves harnessed to. Yes, the salesman admits, it is all very convoluted, but if the knowledge can be mastered, it will serve us well throughout life. The Second Self buys into the sales pitch. He is convinced that he must achieve a clear understanding of this knowledge and that he must learn to skillfully put that knowledge to practical use. The salesman assures him that it is his only hope for acceptance and survival in the established social structure.

The Second Self becomes our impostor. He is created by a social-indoctrination process that every one of us is subjected to. He is complicated, troubled and troublesome, full of anxiety, driven by a complex, often contradictory code of morality, and is prone to self-flagellation as penance for his clandestine enjoyment of "sins" committed by his pleasure-seeking Original Self. Yet, it is this Second Self that is essential for survival in the world that our species has created for itself. The telling of our first lie is a clear indication that the indoctrination, the brainwashing, is on its way to successfully producing the socially desired product.

The Second Self has two main objectives. Number one has to do with policing and concealment of the Original Self. This involves restraining the Original Self from committing behaviors that are deemed socially unacceptable, morally wrong, or decisively evil. This is always a difficult task, sometimes an impossible one. When it is impossible, the Second Self is responsible for coming up with lies to cover up or rationalize these unacceptable behaviors. It is crucial for the Second Self to achieve this primary objective, at least on a fairly consistent basis, to have any hope of achieving his number two objective.

The number two objective has to do with assuring acceptance into society by way of a total submission to the herd mentality. This has to do with conforming to predetermined social expectations. It also requires successful affiliation with organizations and belief systems that are appropriate to one's culture and one's particular social status. It is true that social structures across the world vary somewhat in their general expectations, but the requirement for submission and conformity is always the same.

Now, the Original Self has no understanding and no interest in understanding right, wrong, what is good, or what is evil. He does not care, even in the slightest, about being accepted by others. He cares even less about the expectations or demands of any social structure. He is only concerned with the immediate gratification of his needs, survival of his biological being, and propagation of his seed. So, in the end, we have two persons living in the same body. We have the Original Self, who is holding his ground as the real and natural being. And we have the Second Self, who is moving toward becoming a social being in order to gain social acceptance. This causes a constant friction, an ongoing battle for control, which will last a lifetime. The only hope for any peace will be in death.

PART II

The ability to lie is an important and everyday aspect of our lives. And yes, a certain level of skill in this area is vital in order to function successfully in society. Lies are handy for placating those we care about so that we do not upset them or hurt their feelings. They are often necessary to ingratiate ourselves with people whom we may not particularly like in order to gain advantage or privilege. They will definitely be necessary to cover up all the other minor and major sins that we will surely commit in our lifetimes. Some of those sins will be motivated by our learned commitment to social expectations. An example would be the shaming and ostracizing of someone because they do not agree with our beliefs. Another common one is the murdering of other human beings over disagreements about ideologies, borders, or resources and then vindicating our behavior by calling it War. These questionable behaviors, and many others, are considered acceptable, even expected, by most societies. But they are only acceptable because of our elaborate skills of deception and illusion that allow us to lie to others and ourselves, thereby saving us from having to face the reality of our actions. We like to think that we possess a moral compass. But that conglomeration of moral perplexity that we call our conscience more often than not leads us astray. And worst of all, our conscience has no capacity for rationalizing and justifying so that we can live with our wicked behaviors—only lies can do that.

It is no surprise that lying is our first sin. It is essential and it requires much practice, so to reach proficiency, it must start early on. Lies are the foundation and the building blocks of our present perception of the world, of our consciousness. That consciousness pivots on the loose, often-changing, interpretations of our reality, which are skillfully manipulated and presented to us by our most skilled liars. Such liars include but are not limited to: world leaders (from brutal dictators to snowflake liberal heads of state), upper-, middle-, and low-level politicians (without exception), therapists of any kind, most educators, solicitors and barristers, marketing specialists, and all religious leaders (most notably the charismatic variety). These highly skilled liars represent a rather small percentage of the human population. I think of these folks as career liars. These are people who lack certain emotions, especially empathy, and most certainly sympathy. This frees them up to lie without restraint and without concern for the damage that their lies may inflict on others. They can present their lies with such convincing conviction that they can sell even the most outrageous falsehoods. These include our leaders. A frightful thought, but one that should not be surprising if we simply review the horrific events that make up human history.

Most of us do not reach the level of these professional illusionists. That is not to say that we do not possess an impressive and highly functional skill level when it comes to lying. We do. But we, the majority, constitute the masses that are notorious for being followers. Followers are very susceptible to other people's lies and do their best lying when they lie to themselves. We let other people's lies become our lies. We repeat to ourselves the lies that we are told, some that make no sense whatsoever, until those lies are totally incorporated into our personal belief system, at which point the lies become our truth. We often become advocates for these lies (our new truth), spreading them by sharing them with anyone and everyone who will listen, sometimes even forcing them on those who are too weak to fend us off. There is a great danger in this, especially if the lies being spread have a potential to ignite destructive action. We see this in far-right or far-left political groups, fanatical religious groups, militia groups, terrorist organizations, and even in sports hooliganism where somehow people forget that "It's just a game, for God's sake." We are so accustomed to lying that we lie to ourselves, our co-workers, our families, and even our children just for the sake of making ourselves feel better, to gain even the slightest boost to our social status, to gain affection that we may or may not deserve, or to control others who are under our care or authority. Lying has become so integral to the mental workings and social life of the typical human being that we become oblivious to the fact that we are the perpetuators and often the victims of our own lies.

All of this may sound a little Freudian. But Freud gave the id (Original Self) a bad rep for being its natural self, for being an animal. He then glorified the ego and the superego (collectively the Second Self) for attempting to double-team the id into submission and for working double time contributing to the socialization of man. That Freudian slant on things works, but only because we have convinced ourselves (perhaps lied, again, to ourselves) that living our lives as impostors in this make-believe world that we have created is somehow a good thing. It makes one wonder if the changes to man's cerebral organ, which occurred during his evolution, were the result of a mistake caused by a genetic mishap. Did that mishap result in a deformity of the human brain that has left us with a malfunctioning consciousness which distorts reality? Doesn't it seem that this false reality, pregnant with delusions of grandeur which support our concept of self-importance, is carrying us to our own destruction? Has that error led us onto a branch of the evolutionary tree that ends in extinction? Maybe, just maybe, our so-called advanced intellect is really the symptom of that brain abnormality rather than the gift we proclaim it to be. Without it, we would not be living an existence that we constantly have to convince ourselves is productive when it is obviously destructive. Maybe we would be living in a real world as our original and natural selves in harmony with nature. Yes, we would face hardships, as all animals do, but we would be free from these distortions of reality, free from self-denial, free from the lies and all the misery they cause.

PART III

There is one other insight related to this whole business of lying, of right and wrong, and of good and evil that I am reluctant to discuss, but it simply refuses to be ignored. It goes back to the beginning, to that first lie. I am a bit apprehensive as I start to write the following words. I feel as if I am about to reveal a secret that will do some great emotional or psychological harm to myself and others. Yet, I know it is not a secret; it is something so obvious that it is impossible not to know. It may fall into the category of a shared trauma, something that we all experience and that we all block out so we do not have to face the truth about things we hold sacred.

To be more specific, it has to do with what motivated and who facilitated that first sin, that first exposure to evil. Were we really all alone, as a two- or three-year-old child, facing that demon of a salesman, or was there someone else there, someone encouraging us and finally convincing us to buy into the sales pitch? Did someone else have a hand in introducing us to sin and initiating the split in our being that would result in a lifetime of constant internal turmoil? I think we all know that there was.

The names of those who took advantage of our innocence and led us to sin, who gave our souls to the devil without our informed consent, are not easily accessible. Those names are buried in the dark recesses of our subconscious. Our own minds have put up a variety of defensive walls to protect the names of the guilty. It requires not only determination but also emotional fortitude to breach these internal fortifications. There is a reason why this tidbit of sensitive information is hidden so well and defended so vigorously. To acknowledge, to speak the names of those who ushered us into sin, may be too shocking, too confusing, too emotionally painful for our minds and our hearts to handle. Even when we have identified the guilty and try to speak their names, an uncomfortable pressure builds that causes our throats to swell, cutting off the words before they can reach our voice boxes.

The attempt to bring forth those names summons up that memory of our first lie. We are forced back into the mind of our two- or three-year-old selves. There we were, still our Original Selves, before the knowledge of right and wrong, good and evil. At that age, it may have seemed to others that we had made some progress toward socialization, or at least domestication, but it was not so. This was evidenced by the fact that we still enjoyed the glorious sensation of eliminating bladder and bowel at will and only resorted to the potty under persistent persuasion. Our hunter-gatherer instinct was still fully activated, forcing us to investigate anything that moved, especially if it ran from us. And we were not content until we caught it and shoved it into our mouths to determine if it was edible. We still had that unbridled, intense sense of competition that forced us to exert dominance over any younger siblings, or even older ones if we were strong enough. We pushed them down or out of the way simply to be ahead of them. We stole their food right from their plate, not because we wanted the food but in hopes of starving them. If the occasion presented itself, we would even make an attempt at out-and-out siblicide so as to eliminate any rivals. Luckily, at that early age, we lacked the strength, physical coordination, or planning skills to be successful. The best we could do was give our siblings a solid thrashing from time to time, just to remind them of their place. This often got cut short by the yelling and screaming of the victims, which alerted others that help was needed. Competition was very important to us at that age because the survival instinct was our driving force. It constantly reminded us that our continued existence was totally dependent on the support and the resources available to us. Anything that competed for that support and those resources was a potential threat to our survival.

All seemed to be going well. Then, just when we were getting a grasp on language skills, certain strange questions appeared from nowhere, catching us more than a little off guard. These were not the typical straightforward questions that we were accustomed to, such as: do you want peas or corn; do you want to play with this toy or that toy? These inquiries were complex and confusing, causing us to feel a bit queasy in our stomachs. That touch of anxiety was alerting us to the danger hidden in these unusual questions. It was at that moment that the salesman appeared at the door, burning holes in our brains with those snake eyes. When he started his pitch, we were still being distracted by those voices repeating those questions. We looked toward the distraction, and there before us we saw the salesman's assistants, the facilitators of corruption, the ushers who would take us from our innocence and lead us to sin and turmoil. Staring at them, in disbelief, we felt their names finally regurgitating up to that place in our throats where we had to vomit them out or else choke. We gagged, and our eyes bulged as we coughed up their names—Mother . . . Father? Yes! It was *our parents* who were presenting those cryptic queries. We knew by their affect that they did not want honest answers to their questions; they wanted the answers that would please them. They were encouraging us to give in to the devil's sales pitch; they wanted us to sin—to lie. The most sinister part of all this was that they knew their demand for us to please them was the equivalent of an ultimatum. In our two-year-old mind, a failure to respond with a lie could jeopardize the continuation of their affection and with it the provision of necessary resources. This was more than a frightful thought for a small child—it was terrifying. Our survival instinct could not tolerate such a threat, so we were left with little choice. The salesman was still rattling on while our parents' questions served as encouragements to submit to the devil's will. Finally, we committed the sin—we lied, hoping our parents would be pleased and the salesman would desist. As soon as the lie slipped from our lips, there was a silence, unnerving at first. The salesman had disappeared. Our parents were overjoyed with our response, and they reassured us of their affection. In turn, we were reassured of survival, as long as we continued to lie.

The visual of our parents' presence in that moment, committing that betrayal, was so shocking to our young minds that we literally blacked the entire episode out. Our survival instinct did its best to prevent major trauma by snatching up the memory, dragging it down into our subconscious, and placing it in a cerebral vault. This same vault will, in our lifetime, be filled with other realities too difficult to face and transgressions too great for self-forgiveness.

PART IV

So, what might those questions be that our parents asked that served so well the devil's purpose? Though they vary in content, they are easily recognizable since they all share one of two identifying characteristics. One, they are questions that demand answers far beyond the mental capacity of a child, yet they are being asked of a child. Or, two, they are questions with answers that if given honestly would be in direct conflict with the norms of the established social structure that the parents are enslaved to and the child is born into.

An example of the first would be something like, "You believe in God, don't you, little Johnny?" The desired (required) answer from the child is the lie. The child senses what his mother wants him to say. He recognizes the ultimatum and the threat to his survival, so his coerced answer is, "Yes, Mommy, I believe in God." The honest, more appropriate answer, though I have taken the liberty to enhance it a bit, would be as follows: "Well, uh . . . no Mommy, can't say I do believe in a god. Aren't you aware that it takes twenty to twenty-five years for the human brain to fully develop? Since I am only two, what would make you think that I have the mental wherewithal to understand the complexities of an abstract like God? I'm beginning to wonder if *your* brain is fully developed. Should you be responsible for a child if you are asking such idiotic questions? Hell, ask me something more age appropriate, like do I believe in SpongeBob SquarePants?"

An example of the second type of question would be something like, "You love your little sister, don't you? You didn't mean to hurt her, did you, Johnny?" Again, the child senses what the parent wants to hear, so to ensure his continued survival, he lies. "Yes, Daddy, I love little sis and no, I didn't mean to hurt her." The honest answer, colored by that habit I have of embellishing, would be as follows: "Daddy, you should know that at this early stage in life, most of my focus is on personal survival and self-satisfaction. I have no knowledge of what you call emotions, love included. It seems to me that what you are referring to as emotions are just attention-seeking tools used by grownups to get their infantile needs met. Of course, this small insight will be lost to me when I become fully socialized and, yes, like you, I will blow emotions up into something they are not—just more lies. But for now, my answer is an honest, No! I don't love my sister. And as far as not wanting to hurt her, I can only offer you the unvarnished truth, which is that I would throw her in front of a minivan for a bag of Skittles."

Before children are forced to deny their Original Selves, honesty simply flows from them. When they speak the truth, it is usually in its rawest form. We, members of the social herd, find such truth shocking and frightening. It threatens the stability of our self-created society and, if not placed in check, can undermine our way of life. The process of socialization emphasizes the importance of lying. It too emphasizes the dangers of honesty, which leaves us with an extreme aversion to veracity. A child sitting in a living room full of company turns to a stranger and, with her little face scrunched up, says, "You stink. You smell like butt." All the adults in the room are aware that the person was having trouble controlling his flatus, but they were utilizing various avoidance and distraction techniques to maintain the lie that nothing was happening.

When the child states the obvious truth, a chain reaction of defense mechanisms kicks into play: people are embarrassed; some try to joke it off; some excuse themselves from the room; apologies as well as excuses are made for the truth being told; and, of course, the child is chastised. These disproportionate reactions illustrate that extreme aversion to truth, even in its smallest and most innocent forms. I must note here that people with certain intellectual limitations will not understand the above example. You know you are one of those people if competitive farting is your favorite party game.

All of us have witnessed similar versions of small children speaking the unfiltered truth before social indoctrination restrained the Original Self. And most of us have witnessed the first lies of a child, or at least their early stages of lying. Many of us can remember feeling pangs of guilt through association. We sympathized with that uneasiness we saw in the child as he struggled to master the skill. Many of us found it so uncomfortable to watch that a voice in our heads was screaming, "Stop! Stop!" But in the end, due to our lack of courage, we said nothing. We may have even tried to smile, to assure the parents that we shared in their enthusiasm as they nudged the little one into sin. It is impossible to deny our complicity in such situations. We always wonder if we could have prevented that first bite of the fruit from the tree of knowledge.

CONCLUSION

I have tried to convince myself that parents in general, but especially my own, had some acceptable reason for being in cahoots with the devil. Wasn't he (the devil) the thing that they were supposed to protect me from? Wasn't their job to lead me in the direction of good and away from evil? Weren't they the same people who told me, till their dying day, that lying was a sin? I asked myself if parents were somehow unaware of the impact their behavior was having on their child, but then I recalled the sight of a child being coaxed into his first lies. The fact that something was being forced, that harm was being done, is just too blatant. There was no question that the child was struggling. There was an unmistakable air of trepidation that radiated from him. Like a puppy that had been scolded or beaten, he frantically looked around for any possible escape as his body literally trembled. There was a heart-wrenching plea in his eyes, but no quarter was given as the parents continued with those questions that demanded a sin, a lie.

Somewhere in my search to understand this phenomenon, I realized that this goes back much further than our parents. This goes back to long ago, to that evolutionary brain change, that neurological reorganization, which eventually changed our perception of ourselves and our world. Our simple acceptance of the fact that we were part of nature was erased and replaced with the delusion that we were separate from nature. The meager bit of intellect that was afforded to us by those cerebral changes was not much to speak of, but it was just enough to spark the human imagination and to spawn the human ego. With imagination, we left behind living in the real world and began living in a world that only exists in our minds. But because of the limitations of our intellect, we were not able to recognize the fact that the world we perceived was *only* imagination. It was all lies, very convincing lies that supported the fallacy of our importance. In our fanciful imagination, we have elevated ourselves to the level of demigods when we are really more like monkeys, who happen to be wearing suits. We have created and recreated our world to accommodate ourselves, without the slightest awareness or concern for all the lies, contradictions, and confusion we have incorporated into our daily existence.

The state of awareness that we believe to be reality is a collection of false perceptions (hallucinations), illusions, delusions, and blatant deceptions. It is the equivalent of a psychosis caused by that evolutionary slip up, that cerebral modification, that deformity of our brain. Like a faulty gene set that has the characteristics of a viral infection, it has infiltrated the DNA of the entire herd, causing a shared psychosis that we have ignorantly nurtured from generation to generation for thousands of years. And it is this thought, this belief, that allows me to forgive my parents for their act of betrayal. They obviously were NGRI (Not Guilty by Reason of Insanity). I think we can all agree that you cannot hold people responsible for their actions if they are psychotic. And I am confident that they were, they are, afflicted with this illness that so flimsily holds our social structure together and affects every one of its members.

And just when I was finding some comfort in my conclusions, I passed by one of those mental mirrors that forces you to reflect your conclusions upon yourself. A truth slowly snuck up on me, causing my mouth to dry and my stomach to tighten, then twist. I had to say to myself that if this shared psychosis is universal, as I have proposed, then I too must be affected. I mean, I am a member of the social herd, a barely functioning member, but still a member. My DNA must be infected with that same faulty gene set that I believe afflicts the entire herd. Then suddenly I felt ashamed, overcome with guilt when I realized that while in the depths of my own psychosis, I too had betrayed my children and given them up to the devil. The shock of this personal revelation was carrying me into the depth of a dangerous depression, but I saved myself before it was too late by finding solace and redemption in the only way possible. I labeled myself as I had labeled my parents—NGRI.

Retransformation

I stood high on Afton Mountain and watched the ghost of night's deep chill. It billowed up as clouds of vapor from the vale. Like a floor that spread before me, it reached from peak to peak, convincing me that clouds could support my mortal feet. It seemed so sure I placed my foot upon it—I thought on it I'd walk. But when I tried, I fell, then took to wing as if I were a hawk. I soared to heights that tempted fate, but before I burned my wings, I dove, and when Saint Peter blinked, I flew through heaven's gate.

I flew past rows of vacant mansions and down endless golden streets, searching for those residents who had found eternal peace. I found them packed together, floating prostrate in a galactic space, staring down into hell as a reminder to keep the faith. A cosmic current carried that sea of souls toward a distant site where God revealed his face in a supernova's light. Beneath the glare—a black hole—which led to Lord knows where. It swallowed up the bewildered souls as they tumbled off the edge.

That Niagara of the faithful did not diminish the sea. It was replenished by new arrivals, who kissed Saint Peter's feet. They were unaware of those before them who floated toward the brink and those who now in free fall fell to unknown fates. Those falling souls pierced the Event Horizon as they neared the speed of light. Time altered, and for a moment they possessed a god-like sight, revealing the truth of creation and of God's origination. By way of spaghettification and then disintegration, the souls completed their retransformation to atomic seed.

This retransformation's conclusion was a Helium-3 fusion—a detonation that freed the atomic seed from singularity's gravitational resolution. Floating free in infinite space, these seeds coalesced to form molecular clouds that stretched as far as a million square miles. These clouds formed a nebula that formed pillars of creation that swirled into a spiral shape that led to star, then planetary formations. A yellow dwarf took its place and relied on gravitational persuasion to keep the planets moving in their proper rotation.

This heliocentric configuration in the Traingulum Constellation represented a routine phenomenon of celestial nature. From here I spied the Milky Way, a faint light in the sky that flickered then flashed, exploded then collapsed, leaving a white dwarf drifting in space destined to vanish in Sagittarius A*.

The remains of life (atomic seed) had traveled trillions of miles from earth for the sole purpose of participating in this new solar system's birth. It took billions of years to become stable and for one of the planets to become able to provide the conditions just right for the seed to spark the start of life.

And so began the process that would lead to the evolution of man, a process controlled by God's hand, which he had duplicated again and again. The motivation was rooted in God's addiction to gambling with Satan on predictions of how long humans would take to turn paradise into uninhabitable waste.

Jaded by this realization, I lit upon a craggy crest. I used my wings to make a nest and there laid my head to rest. I woke to find my immortality and my wings repossessed. I had transformed into a primitive man who carried a bone-tipped spear and a stone ax in his hands. I wore the skins of my victims, whose pelts held the cold at bay, as I struggled to remain a predator and not become the prey.

Once again, I stood high on a mountaintop and watched the ghost of night's deep chill. It billowed up as clouds of vapor from the vale. Like a floor that spread before me, it reached from peak to peak, convincing me that clouds could support my mortal feet. It seemed so sure I placed my foot upon it—but then I changed my mind. Now that I knew the truth, I thought I'd bide my time.

What need is there to hurry down a path that has no end and only circles back to where it first began? What need is there to fear fate or sacrifice myself for faith? What need is there for dreams or aspirations, when mankind's evolution only serves to satisfy his suicidal nature? What need is there to fear death when my essence, atomic seed, will be transported into eternity? Far better that I accept my role as a pawn in an endless game—whose only purpose is to entertain.

Doggone Lonely

PART I

Back in the early seventies, I used to chill out with Gary, a friend of mine who lived on the bottom floor of one of those old foursquares in South Norfolk. We often smoked reefer until our drug-induced paranoia convinced us that the neighbors were about to call the fire department to report the smoke billowing out of Gary's bedroom window. We loved to listen to Three Dog Night when we got high and often left "Mama Told Me Not to Come" blasting on the stereo in that smoke-filled room while we took breaks out on the front porch.

I remember how much I enjoyed sitting out there, elevated five feet or more off the ground. It gave us sort of a bird's eye view of our surroundings. It was especially pleasant on cool fall days, wrapped in a warm coat, drinking cold beer that Gary's dad had left unguarded in the refrigerator. At that time, South Norfolk was home to a variety of characters who were far more interesting to watch than anything you could find on the boob tube. We would sit there, on that raised porch, enjoying our high while being entertained by the goings-on of the local inhabitants.

One of the regulars was an older woman, whom we affectionately nicknamed Loosey Lucy. Whenever we saw her, she was alone. And from our understanding, she had always been alone. She dressed and carried herself as you would expect of a proud woman who survived on a limited income. She spoke to people as they passed and conversed with a few people she knew from the neighborhood. She seemed normal. But through a crack in her facade of normality seeped out an abnormality. What caused the abnormality or the crack was never known. It was at first just an odd behavior, something folks snickered at when Lucy's back was turned. But this peculiarity grew and expanded, becoming a preoccupation that eventually consumed her.

Lucy's idiosyncrasy began when she acquired a pet. More specifically, it had to do with the way she related to her pet. The animal was a creature difficult to describe. The first time Gary and I saw the thing, we looked at each other and in the same instant said—"Dog?"—not being quite sure what species it belonged to. After much thought, Gary and I came up with the only logical explanation for this creature's existence. One of those giant-ass wharf rats from the downtown waterfront must have cornered a Chihuahua, had its way with it, and thereby created this miniature Frankenstein. Luckily for the creature, Lucy was a little loose in the head, because only a crazy person could love this thing. It was a little bulkier than you would expect, like a Chihuahua on steroids, but still short in stature, being no more than seven or eight inches tall. Its face resembled a rat more than a dog, which gave it a bit of a demonic look. If its ears had been just a little bigger, they could have belonged to a mule deer. On his forehead was a patch of hair that stood straight up, making the thing look like it was surprised, all the time, and there was a tuft at the very end of its tail. Other than that, it was bald.

In the beginning, Lucy walked him on a thin leash. He was stupid or possibly suicidal, which was understandable if he had ever caught a good look at himself in a mirror. He pulled on the leash as if he was imitating an Alaskan Husky trying to pull a thousand-pound sled until he literally choked himself out. He'd lie there with his tongue hanging out, not breathing for a second or two, then suddenly start gasping for breath. It took him a good five minutes to recover, then he was back up pulling on the leash again, repeating the entire process. Thank God that didn't go on very long—it was hard to watch. Lucy soon stopped walking the thing and started carrying it around. She carried it as one would carry a baby, you know, kind of cradling it in her arms. Being held in this manner was unnatural for a rat or a dog, so the thing resisted for a while, but finally gave up when it realized that Lucy's persistence was inexhaustible. She talked to the rat dog as if it were a child. She introduced the thing to others and encouraged others to speak to it, assuring them that it understood whatever was said. At this point, the neighbors really started worrying about Lucy. But she was a part of the community, and no one wanted to be that person who threw the first stone.

Then one day, Loosey Lucy came walking down the block pushing an old worn-out baby carriage. She must have found it in someone's trash, or maybe she got it from some poor excuse of a thrift shop that just didn't give a shit what they sold. And yes, inside the carriage was the rat dog. Lucy had dressed that fucking thing up like a little baby. She had gone to a lot of trouble to make the necessary alterations so the clothes would fit, and I must say that they fit very well. It was in baby pajamas with the feet cut off and the material neatly hemmed. The thing had little socks on its paws (all four). I am not sure, but I think it was wearing a miniature diaper underneath those pj's. A tiny sweater and a little baby's toboggan kept the chill off. The toboggan had holes cut out for those big-ass ears to stick out of. It was impressive, comical, and disturbing all at once.

We saw Lucy a few more times, but community members, finally motivated by a mixture of concern and increasing anxiety, reported Lucy's behavior to the powers that be. Before very long, she was carried off to Eastern State Hospital. She remained confined there until her death some years later. I understand that the police put the rat dog in a burlap bag and tossed it into the Elizabeth River. Apparently, no one could stand to look at it, much less care for it.

PART II

Time passed. I got older, gave up smoking reefer, stopped taking beer out of other folks' refrigerators without asking, and stopped listening to Three Dog Night (or at least not every day). I had not thought about poor old Loosey Lucy for decades. The memory of her seemed to have vanished, as if she had never existed—until one October day, during a visit to Williamsburg, Virginia. Whenever I am there, I enjoy wandering through the restored colonial area. I was sitting on one of those benches down on Duke of Gloucester Street, trying to take in the historical ambiance, when it became painfully clear that the primary function of Colonial Williamsburg had changed. It had once been a premiere historical and educational site, but evidently it had been converted into a full-fledged dog park. All around me, as far as the eye could see, were dogs of every type and every size shitting, pissing, and dragging their itchy asses all over American history. Each of those creatures had in tow at least one, sometimes more, subservient humans that I can best describe as pet-obsessed psychotics. The sight of it brought the memory of old Loosey Lucy back to life. It was as if her spirit had multiplied and taken possession of the thousands who now crowded the streets of our colonial capital.

So strange was this spectacle that I returned the next day to assure myself that someone had not spiked my drink the day before with some type of hallucinogen. But to my great dismay, I had not been drugged. There before me was a world turned upside down, a world where dogs had become the masters of men and the term "pet owner" had become synonymous with "pet's servitor." While watching this circus, I spotted well over a dozen tricked-out baby carriages and a few pull-behind wagons, lined with plush pet pillows to cushion the heinie of what was apparently canine royalty. All the beasts, whether riding in lavish carriages, carried like helpless infants, or prancing on all fours had human servants humbly attending to their every whim. These servants stayed busy applying paw-balm to protect precious paws, positioning umbrellas to divert the harsh rays of the sun, covering their pooches in custom-made doggy blankets if a chill came in the air, filling personalized doggy bowls with brand-named bottled water, and providing snacks, liberally, to appease their beasts.

But the most astonishing task performed by these lackeys was the collection of pet excrement. Whenever the animals showed any sign of needing to defecate, the servants would stand at the ready with a plastic glove on one hand and a bag in the other. Some picked up the stool, examining it closely, as if expecting to find a treasure in the germ-infested excrement. You would think they were chasing behind the goose that laid the golden eggs. It made me shake my head and wonder: how does one's need for humiliation become so great and one's self-esteem so low that it would allow a person to voluntarily and publicly scoop the poop of another creature? The beasts, having been trained to accept what no creature would ever expect, stood patiently as their servants collected and inspected the feces. The servants would then enthusiastically praise the animals for defecating, as if it were not a normal bodily function but rather an acquired skill that the dogs had somehow learned to excel at.

For all their efforts, the servants were rewarded by being demeaned even further. The dogs, often having just completed one of their favorite past times, licking clean their genitalia and anus, would give their lackeys big sloppy kisses, directly in their faces. The servants, so overjoyed by what they perceived as a show of affection from their masters, would laugh hardily, throwing open their mouths and exposing their nostrils to large doses of contaminated saliva from those fecal-coated tongues.

And as if that weren't enough degradation, the dogs, without any warning, would attempt to violate their owners (servants) by treating them like cheap whores. Little dogs attached themselves to their owner's leg and humped away as if hopped up on amphetamines. Their determination to satisfy themselves was so great it required an almost superhuman effort to detach the little deviants. Or there was the more frightening experience of larger dogs releasing their pent-up bisexual passions on their owners. I witnessed attacks where the victims were almost taken to the ground as the animals exerted their best effort to service their owners. This seemed to occur most often when other people were present, as if the dogs were determined to make the indignity as great as possible. If these acts were committed by human beings, they would qualify as felony sexual assault, and the culprits would surely be arrested and jailed. But because these acts were committed by the pet owner's object of adoration, it was tolerated, even accepted, as part of the perverse relationship that exists between pet owners and their beasts.

As I continued to observe, I discovered the true depth of the owner's psychosis. Their illness included the fixed delusion that dogs (especially their own) had a highly evolved intellect and a highly developed emotional capacity. Most owners proclaimed, without any hesitation and in all sincerity, that their pet was much more intelligent than any human they knew and far more capable of having a loving relationship. It made me wonder how these folks acquired such a low opinion of their fellow human beings. But, then again, I guess pet owners have to believe that animals possess some of the more noble human qualities to justify the fact that they have chosen dogs to love—if not damn near worship. The relationships that these owners have with their pets is akin to the relationships that overzealous parents have with their children. But there is more to it than just that. These relationships too have aspects that one would imagine in fantasy friendships. For example, pets serve as constant, inexhaustible sources of emotional support: pets always agree, or should I say they never disagree, with anything the owners say or do, and they accept their owners unconditionally, oblivious to all the owner's faults and shortcomings. Owners also live with the delusion that their pets can fully understand human languages and have special powers that allow them to communicate their doggy thoughts directly into their owners' minds. Owners can be observed constantly responding to auditory hallucinations that they chalk up to their pet's telepathic powers of communication. This is a common feature with this particular mental disorder.

With consideration to all the above, I must forewarn non–pet owners that the well-known protective instinct that folks have for their children and their friends is fully present when it comes to owners and their pets. If you don't believe me, just insult the intellect or emotional capacity of someone's pet, question the dog's ability to communicate, or move someone's intrusive canine away from you by giving it a good nudge with your foot. I can guarantee you; the shit will hit the fan.

I also overheard many conversations between these psychotic pet owners that revealed a twisted pride related to the cost of maintaining their pet and the sacrifices that it required. It was like listening to martyrs competing by comparing the concessions they had made and the suffering they had endured so their pet could enjoy the lifestyle that it so richly desired. They also talked in detail about the dozens of books they had read and the social networks they belonged to in an effort to keep current with the most recent fads related to pet care. It was obvious that this pet obsession was not an isolated phenomenon, occurring just in Williamsburg. It was nationwide.

PART III

I discovered that there is a one-hundred-billion-dollar pet market out there, encouraging and supporting this obsession. Every type of fraud, quack, and flimflam artist imaginable has smelled the blood in the water. They have jumped on this moneymaker and are busy committing all types of skulduggery in their effort to suck every last dollar out of the pockets of these mentally incompetent, emotionally vulnerable, yet somehow socially functional pet owners. These bloodsucking opportunists have become so efficient at taking advantage of this pandemic of mental illness that they have created a sort of alternative reality for pet owners. It is a reality where the value of a beast has become equivalent to, if not greater than, any person. I find it beyond queer that humans would choose to worship a creature that has the shocking, yet impressive, ability to lick its own testicles, cannot resist putting its nose up the ass of other creatures, and that from time to time has been known to eat its own shit. But there it is.

I am told by pet owners that most days for their four-legged deities begin with having their fur as well as their teeth brushed. A bit of pet deodorant and few drops of expensive pet perfume may be applied. Breakfast is served in expensive bowls, adorned with hand-painted scenes of puppies frolicking in a park setting. The food served is usually more expensive by the pound than anything else found on the family's grocery list. But even so, it is thrown away if not eaten immediately—his majesty certainly cannot be expected to eat leftovers. While the animal partakes of its gourmet meal, its calendar is checked for planned events and appointments. Finally, the animal is dressed appropriately to suit its schedule and the weather.

I was shocked when I realized the variety of clothing items and accessories available for a dog—from pajamas to tuxedos, from skull caps to tiaras, costumes of various types for every holiday, jewelry, scarves, and, yes, doggie diapers. You will occasionally see dogs in jumpsuits, but their most preferred style is upscale casual, routinely complemented with a classy sweater or jacket. They of course wear raincoats and waterproof booties in inclement weather. On sunny days, you may see dogs treated as the honored guests on family boats, wearing wetsuits and goggles or, perhaps, brightly colored life jackets. They sport bandannas of different colors and patterns, sunglasses with decorative frames, and for the really cool canine, a pair of black-framed Blues Brothers shades. I bet Loosey Lucy is sitting up in heaven with a big old smile on her face.

After being primped, pampered, and dressed, the pet is ready to start its busy day. It may be dropped off at school (training class) followed by an afternoon at the pet salon for a shampoo, ear cleaning, and pawdicure. Or perhaps it is off to day care for a bit of romping and socializing, then snacking and napping with peers who also wallow in the benefits of their pet privilege. Then there are those regularly scheduled sessions with the pet therapist. On these days, the owner must be sure the pet is wearing its made-to-order anxiety jacket. Occasionally an owner will make the mistake of asking how therapy is going. They are given a firm reminder about the rules of confidentiality—what happens in therapy stays in therapy—which leaves the owner more than a little embarrassed for having asked. The owner doesn't really know what they're paying for, but the therapist assures them that the sessions are necessary for the pet's mental health and emotional well-being (whatever that means). Some days are spent shopping for that perfect birthday gift for a doggy buddy whose special day is coming up. There will be a splendid party with banners, balloons, party hats, hired entertainment in the backyard, a delicious cake made of beef pâté and sprinkled with crushed doggy treats. To top it all off, everyone will leave with a gift bag containing the best-quality bully sticks (dried bull penises) in assorted flavors.

Then there are those dreaded visits to the "Pet Care Professionals" who have convinced the pet owners that their dogs have no chance of survival unless thousands of dollars are spent annually on health care. An owner will occasionally wonder about their parents' old work dogs. Those animals, who not only endured but seemed to relish in the demands of farm life, lived to be damned near ancient without ever seeing the inside of a vet's office. But these thoughts are erased when the care professional shares a few horror stories of what happened to pets when callous owners denied the animal this shot or that treatment. From time to time, even a surgery may be necessary or, more likely, recommended. Some of the most common pet surgeries include dental, orthopedic, cataract, spinal, amputation, and spaying or neutering. The collective cost of general medical care, coupled with a surgery or two, can eventually challenge the stability of an owner's financial status. But somehow owners manage to find the funds. Often those funds can be traced back to second mortgages, depleted college funds, or diminished retirement saving accounts.

There are certain products and procedures reserved for only the most gullible, such as silicone testicle implants—brand name Neuticles. This often involves a conspiracy of sorts between pet service providers. FYI, such conspiracies are much more common than anyone would imagine. It works something like this. First the pet's medical specialist advises an owner to have their dog neutered. When that is done, they kick the owner over to a pet therapist who schedules weekly appointments (which are as expensive as the monthly payment on a good used car) to help the dog deal with the trauma of having had his balls cut off. After a serious evaluation of the pet's mental status (really), the therapist kicks the owner back to the medical specialist with a recommendation for the dog to have testicle implants. The therapist assures the owner that this is necessary to decrease the animal's high anxiety level caused by the loss of his balls and to aid the beast in re-establishing a healthy self-image (I swear, I am not making this shit up). The medical specialist completes the procedure, which of course calls for multiple and costly follow-up appointments, then kicks the owner back over to the pet therapist to assure that the animal is adjusting psychologically to his balls mysteriously *reappearing*. Are you dizzy yet? I am, and that is just one of the hundreds of games played in that alternative reality that pet owners live in.

It is strange to think that, in this day and time, health insurance and life insurance is purchased for a pet just as it is for a spouse or for one's child. It is also becoming more and more common for the funeral ceremonies of a pet to be so elaborate that it is indistinguishable from that of a beloved human family member. Although a conjecture on my part, I believe that many pet owners spend much more on their pets annually than they give to charities or even to God's work if they have a religious leaning.

While millions of fellow human beings suffer and die each year due to a lack of basic resources, millions of pets luxuriate in lavish lifestyles usually reserved for nobility. And it is this sobering thought that forces me to withdraw from my ramblings and ask myself this serious question. What the fuck has happened that allowed this madness to fit into our framework of normality?

PART IV

The answer to that question is not as complicated as it may at first seem. The simple fact is that the social conscience of any group is extremely pliable as it relates to what constitutes normal versus abnormal. If a certain percentage of the total population, voluntarily and routinely, becomes engaged in a particular behavior, then that behavior, even if it was previously considered abnormal, will come to be accepted as normal. This acceptance of a new normal can be triggered by a majority agreement, or even by a minority if that minority is made up of the more assertive people in the group. When the minority of a population institutes a new norm by the sheer power of assertiveness, it is always because the majority, who opposed the behavior, remained silent. In other words, the assertive voice of the few, which meets no resistance, soon becomes the voice of the whole. There is more that can be said on this subject, but this will suffice for now, as I find myself distracted by a much more intriguing question.

You may think that question is: What could cause such a strange psychosis supported by such outrageous anthropomorphic delusions? But no, psychosis has been around forever, and the characteristics of psychosis vary greatly from case to case and are quite often bizarre. The really interesting question here is, how can a psychosis, with identical features, afflict enormous numbers of unrelated human beings across an entire nation? If this madness were a virus, it would make sense that we are surrounded by hordes of dog-obsessed psychotics, but there is no data that suggests mental illness is contagious.

Finally, it dawned on me. This is an emotional crisis so pervasive that it could only be caused by some major social disturbance. The obsessions, delusions, and irrational behaviors of pet owners are not the illness but rather symptoms of the illness, and that illness is Loneliness. Now, you will not find Loneliness in the DSM-5, or even in the *Merck Manual*, but that does not change what most of us know. We know that periods of aloneness can be appreciated as welcomed states of tranquility, but only if one has very definite control over the initiation and termination of the experience. Aloneness uncontrolled can morph into Loneliness, a painful emotional state that if prolonged can become life threatening. Loneliness shares some characteristics with major depression, one of our most popular modern-day diagnoses. But Loneliness should not be mistaken for depression. At most, depression is but one of the symptoms associated with what should accurately be diagnosed as "Severe Loneliness with Psychotic Features."

This disorder is very distressing since Loneliness and Death have an intimate connection to one another. They both stir up the same sense of desperation. Dealing with one always forces us to eventually deal with the other. We humans are intensely aware of this connection, if not on a cognitive level, then on an instinctual or possibly metaphysical level. After all, coming to terms with profound Loneliness is part of preparing ourselves for Death. It demands that we accept the separation of ourselves from everyone and everything we have known while mustering up the courage to face, alone, a pending unknown. Somewhere in each of us, we fear that Death is Loneliness, unmitigated and inescapable. Loneliness is most often viewed as a horrifying event, like Death, which we try to avoid at all costs. When personal or social circumstances place us in the ominous state of Loneliness, or even threaten to do so, our reactions can be and often are extreme—very extreme. You just never know what behaviors you may display or what act you may commit to escape the horror of it.

PART V

Following that train of thought, the next logical question is: What changes in our social makeup caused this pandemic of Loneliness? Now, I am not a social scientist or a historian by profession. But I have read a considerable amount of history and have a good grasp of the concepts surrounding social change. I think everyone agrees that social change is always afoot and that certain periods in history are representative of major and specific transition. The change I am concerned with here has to do with the breakdown of American society's most basic structural components, the family unit and small community. The rumblings of this social transformation began with the Industrial Age in the late 1700s. The change began to show itself throughout the 1800s and into the twentieth century. The collapse of these traditional social components accelerated after World War II and has since continued at a steady pace. It has left many, if not most of us, with a grim awareness of our emotional detachment from other human beings.

I am aware that the loss of the traditional family unit and, in turn, small communities can be seen as constructive or destructive, depending on one's point of view. Some argue that the loss of such is the primary cause of many, if not all, of our present-day personal and social woes. These folks believe it to be the cause of the general lack of moral character in our citizenry and the corruption that runs rampant through all our social institutions. On the other hand, some see ridding ourselves of family and community ties as an opportunity that has allowed for individual expression and growth. They would say that the elimination of such has freed people from the shackles of worn-out roles, stifling expectations, unwanted responsibilities, and oppressive obligations. I think that both arguments have some validity. But there is no denying that these two interdependent social components were the glue that historically held our society together. So, we must ask ourselves, if the glue that held our society together has been done away with, then what now holds it together? The answer to that question is "nothing." We have not, as of yet, found a replacement for what is lost. Acknowledging this fact places me solidly in the camp of those who believe that the loss of the family unit and small community does indeed constitute a destructive event or rather a destructive result of an event (social change).

PART VI

Family and community once gave people a sense of security, emotional stability, a feeling of belonging, and a profound sense of purpose as well as a set of social expectations that provided structure to their lives. There was an emotional investment in one's family unit that extended itself, in various degrees, to members of one's small community. This arrangement provided emotional support to all involved, not just at one stage of their lives but throughout their lives. There was intimate, direct, daily involvement with others, sharing all the good, the bad, the struggles, the losses, and the victories. This human connection assured the emotional health of the entire family and community. That connection to other human beings has been lost, which is devastating to the human psyche and to our social structure.

It is apparent to me that the absence of those once essential but now devalued components of our society has deprived us of our sense of "we" and left us alone with only our inflated sense of "I." Today it is common to be estranged from parents and siblings, if not by choice, then by distance or by being engrossed in one's occupation. Marriage, once solidified by religious belief and social expectation, has become a flimsy affair that is dispensed with at the slightness whim. Our lack of interest in even bothering with marriage, and the rate of divorce for those who do give it a try, is escalating. Both are likely indicators of our profound preoccupation with self. What about children, who used to be the pride and joy of families and communities? Yes, we continue to produce offspring, but only because we are driven to by primitive instinct rather than by rational intent. In the aftermath, when logic finally sets in, most ask themselves, "What in the world was I thinking?" In today's world, children are often thought of as irritating inconveniences, stumbling blocks that slow the progress of our chosen careers, and financial drains that show little in the way of return. Stuck with them, as we are, we spend much of our lives attempting to relinquish our responsibility for raising them to anyone or any system willing to take them on—relatives, friends, babysitters, au pairs, summer camps, day care providers, preschools, kindergartens, or private schools. Our seniors, traditionally our respected mentors, are now viewed much in the same way we view children: an inconvenience, an encumbrance, and potentially a financial drain. Our biggest hope for them is not for their physical and mental well-being but rather for their financial well-being. There is always that self-centered concern that some ineptness on their part, related to money management, will derail not only their lives but also ours if they should become dependent on our support. And friends, once our lifelong confidants, have been replaced with associates. These are individuals or groups of individuals who provide an exchange of specific services or assure access to something that we desire. Oftentimes, they simply serve the purpose of supporting the views we have of ourselves and the world. These relationships have no real substance, quickly ended and replaced if one or the other fails to meet the spoken or unspoken expectations.

It seems obvious, even if evidenced by nothing more than the emotional shallowness of our society, that true human connection was in fact essential to our emotional development and mental well-being. Without it, we are left to wallow in our narcissism, unable to see beyond our own petty wants and needs—much like whining infants. The desperation we feel from that human disconnect and the absence of emotional support can manifest itself in some unexpected ways (e.g., finding emotional solace in a relationship with a pet). And sadly, or not, depending on your view of things, there seems to be no going back. The "we" culture of the past is being replaced with the "I" culture of the present at a rapid rate. Our preoccupation with self, which can be characterized as a pathological self-love, is now a dominating feature of society, and it is eroding any hope of ever again reuniting with others. We do not have any concept of how to compensate for the loss of human connection. But without that compensation, without a viable alternative, there is nothing to save us from Loneliness.

PART VII

To complicate things even more, the creation of and the advancements in technology, specifically in the area of communications, has been nothing short of mind-boggling. These developments came along at the worst possible time, running parallel with the destruction of the traditional family unit and small community. It all began with one or two people pecking away on a telegraph. Today there are billions pecking away on smartphones, tablets, and laptops. When feelings of detachment were reaching a peak, our society accepted this technology as a replacement for human intimacy. Supporters of these new methods of communication say that it has brought people closer together. They are referring to our ability to relay data almost anywhere on the planet in what is referred to as real time. They mistake this rapid and efficient method of sharing information for true human connection. This expedient exchange, with its abbreviations, emojis, cryptic languages, and superficiality has little to do with the profound emotional exchange that occurs between two people engaged in the living of real life. This can only be experienced through direct physical presence. But in a desperate effort to reconnect to others, most of the population has immersed itself in technology, with a reckless disregard for its obvious negative effects, especially its powerful addictive quality. That all-consuming, 24/7 addiction has deterred us from our primary objective. Instead of solving our problem, it has distracted us from our problem. It fools us mentally into believing that we are experiencing real relationships, but it cannot fool us emotionally. No matter how many hours a day we spend on our devices, that sense of aloneness never leaves us—every time that screen goes blank, there it is. We have become a society of emotionally starved human beings, hypnotized by the flashing screens of our communication tools.

We are hoping beyond all reason that we can replace the touch of a friend's hand or the embrace of a loved one with some binary code that is transported through some fiber-optics using the phenomenon of TIR (total internal reflection). Somehow that just doesn't sound as comforting as a good hug.

CONCLUSION

I wonder how long we will remain in this technology-induced trance. How much time, how many decades will we waste? And I wonder, what will become of it all? Perhaps technology will eventually develop a robotic companion so advanced that it will service our emotional needs in some futuristic way that is presently beyond our imagination. Or perhaps the masses will resign themselves to the inescapable reality of their emotional detachment and simply give up on living. This could result in a culling of the human herd, like that which naturally occurs from time to time with other species. Great numbers could be lost due to mass suicides in a last-ditch effort to escape the pain of Loneliness. These same folks might commit multiple homicides on their way out to vent their rage on cold, detached fellow creatures who were too busy texting to even notice the distress of others. I wonder, when the majority of the population has been done away with, will there be an awakening among the remaining? Will they abandon technology and be forced back to tribal living, back to dependence on one another, back to human connection? Or, perhaps, Loneliness will drive more and more people to turn to animals for some semblance of emotional connection. All SPCAs could be emptied, and the price of a single pet could eventually exceed the annual salary of a corporate executive. Every cent of expendable income and every ounce of our compassion could be squandered on our pets while our sense of humanity withers and world problems are ignored until society finally collapses around us. Who knows what will happen! What we do know is that in the absence of emotionally programmed androids, or until mass suicides and homicides have devastated our population, or until we put aside the whole charade so we can just go ahead and marry our pets, we will be yearning and searching for something to fill that void left by the absence of true human relationships.

And that brings us back to Colonial Williamsburg. I am visiting again and have been wandering about for some time. I am now sitting here in Merchant's Square, taking a break and trying to enjoy my favorite coffee drink (a Dog Street Chill) from my favorite coffee shop (Aromas). While doing so, I am watching a pet owner who is watching his lusus naturae, a.k.a. labradoodle, take a dump by the statue of Thomas Jefferson. I cannot help but think of Albert Camus who said, "The literal meaning of life is whatever you're doing that prevents you from killing yourself." If that means being a servant to a four-legged, hairy fucker who treats you like a piece of shit, well . . . I guess that's better than sticking your head in a gas oven . . . I guess.

I am still irritated by the invasion of this historical ground by hordes of dogs and their insane owners, but I do understand them a little better. I see now that these owners are lonely people, driven by a dire need to love and be loved. They are trying, trying so very hard to find emotional security and that purpose in life that traditionally was provided by their attachment to other human beings. I also have come to understand why that minority, who have not yet been tempted to look for love at the SPCA, tend to ignore or laugh off the bizarre behavior of pet lovers. Their only alternative is to acknowledge the failure of our society. But facing the reality that emotional detachment plagues our nation will do little good if we are unable to turn off our phones long enough to engage the problem-solving aspect of our brains.

I am fortunate that I have one person left in this world who shares my life, who communicates with me, who will hold my hand and embrace me. She does this freely, without being on salary and with only reasonable expectations of reciprocation. I guess this makes me someone who is only one person away from aloneness, which is only a step away from Loneliness, which is less than spitting distance from insanity or death. My greatest fear is that I could lose this most valuable human companion, this one last human connection. Without her, I fear I would find myself staring at the ass of a Rottweiler, whom I have dressed in a yellow tutu with matching ballet slippers, humbly waiting at the ready with a plastic glove on one hand and a bag in the other.

Oneness

Have we humans created a tremendous problem for ourselves by not accepting what we are? What we are is a collection of simple elements—I refer you to the periodic table. Elements constitute matter. Matter constitutes all that we are and all that surrounds us. That is to say that each of us is part and parcel of something much bigger than ourselves. Particular elements have configured themselves into the shape of our present physical being. But, be assured, that state of being is short-lived. Each one of us, in just a very limited span of time, will give back those simple elements to the whole, and they will be used again and again. There is no such thing as death, not as we think of it. That is just a concept generated by fear. What we think of as death is no more than a decomposition followed by a reconfiguration. The possible results of that reconfiguration and the purposes it may serve can number in the millions. They can present themselves in any form, anywhere in the world or in the universe. When the result of that process happens to present as a human being, we refer to it as a birth. It is strange and a little hard to comprehend, but when we witness a birth, we think of it as a new arrival, a new beginning. But in reality, we are witnessing the result of a process as old as time, one that has produced a product that consists of components as old as the cosmos. We should experience an incredible peace in knowing our purpose, in knowing that we are not only a product of but also a contributor to such an amazing process. So why don't we live our lives accordingly?

It is because we have conjured up and now pass on the annoying belief that each of us is a single, unique entity, separate and apart from all other people and all other things. This false belief forces us to imagine that there is an inside of us and an outside of us. But we know better. Whenever we close our eyes and quiet our minds, even for a few seconds, we immediately become aware of a *knowing*, faint and elusive, that dwells in the darkness just behind our eyelids. We want to believe that boundless darkness, full of floating and flashing lights in various configurations, is nothing. But we know that it is the whole, it is everything. We sense it, we know that it surrounds us. We may feel overwhelmed or even swallowed up by it, but only because we struggle to comprehend it, to take it all in. It is too large to fit into any field of vision or even into the limits of the grandest imagination; therefore, we are left blind to it. And because we are blind to the truth, we lose our way.

The truth is replaced by that unfounded belief in oneness that is forced on us at birth, then reinforced throughout life, motivated (I suppose) by some misguided need to make every individual feel special. Isn't it special enough to be a part of all creation? Once that belief is instilled in our being, we become totally convinced that our oneness is the beginning and the end of what we are. This explains our immense phobia of death. We think of death as hitting a wall, as a dead end, a horrible process of disintegration into oblivion. In a desperate effort to ease that fear, which we ourselves have created, we disregard logic and stretch the bounds of sanity by accepting various forms of bizarre afterlife fantasies. These fantasies, some older than the tales of Gilgamesh, originated during a time when mankind's intellect was in its infancy, without an established knowledge base to fend off stories of ghosts and goblins. But even today, with our proudly proclaimed intellectual progress, we cling to beliefs of old mythical gods who sprout wings, then flitter about in cities that float in the sky. We believe in hellish tricksters in devil's drag who tempt us into responding to the darker side of our nature, and then punish us for doing so. We do not hold on to these because they continue to make sense to us, but rather because we are still trying to sooth that horrifying fear of losing our imagined oneness to what we erroneously think is unimaginable nothingness.

Death seems to have evaded all our efforts to understand it. But that is only because we already have the answers, though we may be unable or unwilling to acknowledge them. To understand and accept the reality of death, as stated at the beginning of this piece, we simply have to rid ourselves of that unfounded concept of oneness. We must accept the truth that we are part of the whole and embrace our true purpose. Once that is achieved, all things make sense, all fear dissipates, and we realize that death was simply a figment of our imagination.

The Parent Trap

PART 1

This essay is primarily about people who are parents but should not be parents. I am not saying that it is entirely these people's fault that they end up with children when they shouldn't have children. There are biological and social factors, which will be discussed, that interfere with logical decision making. These factors should be obvious, yet somehow, we fail to acknowledge them and therefore fail to deal with them. My intent is not to blame anyone or any group of people, as the factors in question affect all human beings. I simply offer a certain perspective on the human condition as it relates to reproduction.

But before I expound upon that, it seems pertinent to say a little about people who *are* meant to be parents, people who have a natural inclination for the job, who become parents by choice, not by accident. These are those people who honestly and proudly proclaim that being a parent is their primary goal in life. Their desire to take on this twenty-five-year task is not taken lightly. It represents the foundation of a life plan that requires much discussion, with many decisions to be made and details to be worked out. It is interesting that the word *sacrifice* never comes up in their discussions. Time, effort, and resources are never sacrificed if you are doing what you love. They are aware and accepting of facts that other people try to ignore or refuse to believe. For example, they know that for them to succeed at being *good* parents one or the other partner will have to invest themselves full-time in the parenting role while the other will need to act in an adjunct capacity. Too, they accept that the role of the adjunct will include being the primary breadwinner. Who will play which role is determined by assessing each partner's particular disposition as it relates to day-to-day parenting versus each partner's aptitude and skill set as it relates to potential level of income. Natural parents understand the importance of providing for the family's basic needs, but they are not excessively materialistic. They actually have a fear of excess want, knowing it has the potential for distracting them from their mission. This ability to be content with the basics decreases their stress and increases their happiness by allowing them to focus on their core purpose in life, being parents.

Let me say clearly—there are very few of these people in the world. Such people are special, but I am not saying that these folks will all succeed in being the best parents or produce a well-rounded, decent human being. Shit, life is treacherous. It is expecting a lot for a couple to toe the line all the way to the end of a twenty-five-year mission. They may change, become incompatible, and divorce, lessening the chance that their offspring will become that well-balanced, emotionally stable adult they had hoped for. Too, there is the unpredictability of genetics. Good parents are not miracle workers. For example, they cannot fix a bad roll of the genetic dice that gives rise to a psychopathic personality, to mention just one of hundreds of genetically influenced brain malfunctions. What I am saying, in case it isn't clear, is that there is more to effective parenting than simply playing the role. For parenting to have a high potential for producing the desired product, there must be at least two individuals who are *invested*. They must possess the attributes necessary for the job, they must have the ability to provide for the child's basic needs in a safe and nurturing environment, and at least one must be able to provide full-time care to their offspring.

PART II

Many may be outraged to hear me say that I believe parents whose primary occupation is being unemployed are not good parents. I also believe that people who are regularly employed, but who are single parents, are not good parents. These two groups can take some comfort in knowing that the same is true of parents who both work full-time jobs. Many of these folks will defend their parenting efforts by becoming aggressive and demanding to be recognized as good parents, which certainly doesn't make it true. Some will defensively say that they do well considering their circumstances and some, being more honest, admit that they do the best that they can. But the truth is that frightening people into saying that you are a good parent, or that you are doing well considering your circumstances, or doing the best you can has nothing to do with good parenting, and there is no way to get around that. If you are a parent who does not work and role models for your child a lifestyle of dependency on others, then you are not a good parent. If you are a single parent who works to pay your way and your child's way you might be a responsible adult, but being responsible is only a part of being a good parent. If you are parents in a two-income family where neither of you is available to provide undivided, full-time attention to the care of your child, then you also are not good parents. The common factor with all these folks, whom I have most assuredly offended, is that underneath all their loud outrage, their violent defense of their parenting skills, their sincere attempts to justify their lifestyles, there is a voice that does not lie. That voice constantly reminds them of their inadequacies as parents and that having children was nothing short of a life-altering mistake. Unfortunately, the folks who hear this voice make up the majority of people who are presently parenting children.

I think all parents who shouldn't be parents suffer from what I like to call "parental regret." Psychiatrists would probably say that parental regret, like buyer's remorse, is cognitive dissonance. Maybe so. I, being a little more simpleminded, describe it as having made a major decision without properly thinking it through, then finding yourself in a fucked-up situation that you really want to get out of but just don't know how to get out of. I guess parental regret is like buyer's remorse in some ways. Let's use a timeshare purchase as an example. People are *convinced* to buy into a timeshare. This is done by some fast-talking "timeshare specialist" whose fingertips are stained with nicotine and whose breath reeks of this morning's hair of the dog. People are also *convinced* to buy into parenthood. This is accomplished by a mindless biological instinct to reproduce, encouraged by traditional beliefs that rationalize the continuation of that mindless reproduction. In both cases, it doesn't take long, after the fact, for a person to realize that they never really wanted a timeshare or to be a parent. One soon learns that getting involved with timeshares or parenthood is very much like getting involved with the mafia. It's something that you are always sorry for and the only way to get out of it is to convincingly fake your own death, then live out the rest of your life incognito in some out-of-the-way location.

One difference between timeshares and parenthood is that you are not sold on having children in a single day, which is the typical timeframe allotted for selling a timeshare. You are sold on the idea of parenthood by way of a profound and comprehensive brainwashing session (social indoctrination) that begins at birth and the effects of which last a lifetime.

Many know that they are not parental material, but that sexual drive is so persistent and that brainwashing so thorough that they forge ahead till they eventually trip up and stumble into that parent trap. Within a month or two after the first one is born, their existence is so altered that they do not recognize themselves or their lives. The regret begins to sink in, but that social indoctrination has installed devices to protect the parenting concept. Little voices in their heads tell them that things will calm down, that they are just having a case of the jitters, common among rookie parents. So, against all common sense and without any clear understanding of why, they put another one in the oven. And when that one arrives, it may or may not finally dawn on them that—*No!*—things are not going to calm down, and if it ever does, they will be too old or too worn out to have the life once dreamed of.

Your mind will want to resist this depressing thought. But the truth is that raising children "properly" consumes as much or more time and effort than is commonly required for working two full-time jobs. There will be times, as the children get older, that it may cut back to the equivalent of just one full-time job, but those periods are short-lived and unpredictable due to the many variables in life that you will have no control over.

PART III

It is common for people who are parents but shouldn't be parents to look back and wonder what happened to that old hype that the '70s promised: "You can have it all." Well, that was a lie. It would have been an obvious lie to almost anyone if not for those decades of brainwashing that sold folks on parenthood. What rational person would believe that you can be a really great husband or wife and a really great parent and in addition be a really great student, or employee, or entrepreneur, or artist, or adventurer. You can't. And if you try to have it all, most everything turns out half-assed. You end up living a half-assed life, being a half-assed parent, who raises half-assed kids. Those kids become half-assed adults who also become half-assed parents who then pass on their half-assed lifestyle to the next generation. It is a perpetual process that has contaminated the human population with an excess of half-assed people.

Some who try to have it all but are unable to tolerate the thought of living a half-assed life decide to live in a delusion. In that delusion, they are the paragon of good parenthood. No, they do not give up climbing that career ladder that requires fifty-hour work weeks or spin class three nights a week, or even their regular Friday night out with friends. But they do manage to present as the epitome of parenthood whenever they are able to find a few spare moments to share with their child. Ironically, they often brag about their perfect child, but the truth is that they pay so little attention and see them so seldomly that they probably wouldn't be able to pick them out in a police lineup. They also love to talk about their parenting skills, often giving out advice and throwing around their favorite two words—unconditional love. These two words are really their way of saying that they do not hold their child responsible for anything they do, that they do not enforce any consequences, and that they expect the rest of the world to also put up with their undisciplined brat without complaint. Other than providing for the basic human needs (food, water, shelter, and such) these parents are absent, physically and emotionally. They have simply given up on parenting and escape any guilt for their child neglect by hiding in their delusion. As far as nurturing goes, children of such parents may as well be raised in a Dickensian orphanage. This all works out well for the parents who are freed up to pursue their real interests in life. But it seldom works out well for the kids. Such home environments are the factories that produce our populations of rapscallions, petty criminals, and the occasional psychopath.

Then there are those who can just barely deal with their own personal issues. Having children, for these folks, is a mistake in so many ways. These are people afflicted with profound issues related to low self-esteem, which makes them the perfect victims in abusive relationships. Experiencing such dysfunctional relationships destroys all their hopes for normal adult companionship. They are beaten down and broken individuals who are desperate to resuscitate their egos. In that desperation, there is a yearning for an emotional connection and for a sense of self-worth. It is not uncommon for these folks to commit themselves fully to parenthood, giving up all ambitions, hobbies, and social life to invest themselves into their child's care. They may not be able to give up employment if it is essential to their survival, which is usually the case, but it is most often a menial job that means nothing to them other than making the rent and making groceries. It is never the type of vocation that distracts them from their primary focus, their child. This is not about being a good parent but rather about raising a companion whom they can rely on—someone who will always love them and always be there.

Such individuals forsake the true mission of parenthood. That mission has to do with assisting in the production of a mentally and emotionally mature adult, one who is socially functional and independent, one who loves and respects the parent but who (and here's the clincher) does not *need* the parent. Instead, these parents sabotage their own child's development. They create a kind of sick interdependent relationship. This type of relationship cripples the child emotionally, leaving them dependent on the parent, preventing them from ever reaching a level of maturity that would allow them to take flight and leave the nest. We have all known at least a few of these adult children who never move out of the parents' house. If they do, they never move more than a short drive away, which allows them to spend more time at the parents' residence than at their own. Or they may be the type who seem cursed by an endless array of upsets, failures, and setbacks that repeatedly force them back under the parents' roof. They are those adult children who have an offensive air of entitlement about them as they stroll through the parents' house in boxer shorts and tattered tank tops, even while guests are present, then stand in front of the open refrigerator scarfing down food scraps and drinking out of the milk carton. The guests are shocked and somewhat repulsed by what is obviously parenting gone very, very wrong. But the parent is quick to defend that forty-year-old man or woman who wanders around their home with no apparent responsibilities nor any trace of self-respect. There are always multitudes of excuses and justifications that the parent rattles off. And they never fail to announce, with the greatest of confidence, that some wonderful opportunity is waiting just around the corner for their *child*. But the truth is, everything is just as these parents want it to be. They have created this child who now resides in an adult body and who must always remain a child so that the parent can retain their companion.

Finally, there are those who jump ship. Walking away and simply ignoring the fact that their child or children exist works well when people are young and fully occupied chasing their dreams, moving from one adventure to the next, or climbing that ladder that they hoped would lead to success. But eventually, most are forced to face the fact that their dreams were just grandiose delusions of their own importance and exaggerations of their talents. For those few who do finally achieve something noteworthy, they soon realize that reaching a goal offers only a short-lived exhilaration, not the long-term satisfaction they had hoped for. When age slows these folks down, even by the slightest degree, all the harm they caused to others in the pursuit of selfish want has a way of catching up with them. In their youthful haste they had buried, in a shallow grave, their guilt for deserting the people who loved and depended on them. In time, the ability to suppress those memories weakens, and that guilt resurrects itself. Once revived, it relentlessly plagues them, never allowing for even a moment of peace. Even at the very end of life, it blots out any pleasant thoughts of good times, good deeds, or achievements that could offer a bit of comfort. That guilt is unyielding in its determination to assure that the delinquent parent's last thought is of their greatest sin—abandoning their child. And who knows, maybe that is not the end of it. Maybe a final, more horrifying retribution is waiting beyond the veil.

PART IV

What I have been describing here are some of the various ways parents who should never have been parents deal with their mistake of having children. These are nothing new. They have been in use forever. But around the mid-sixties, a new technique for dealing with parental regret, called early childhood education (ECE), began to emerge. It does not escape my attention that it appeared around the same time that the two-income family was becoming the new norm for middle America, replacing the old, traditional family unit that depended on only one wage earner. The liberation movement had freed womenfolk from housewifery. Females crashed the gates of male-dominated workplaces and soon learned the joys of being emancipated from the drudgery of housework and childcare. And they became addicted to the independence they experienced from making their own weekly paycheck. Some of the more adaptable males could be convinced to do a few household tasks, but most had no desire or intention of taking on any parenting duties. This left both fathers and mothers desperate to find some way to rid themselves of those suffocating parental responsibilities.

Luckily, ECE suited these parents' needs perfectly. It originated from a tenuous concept that evolved into a flimsy theory that eventually found its place in that collection of accepted but faulty ideas known as common knowledge. It is based on the feeble hypothesis that introducing children, as early as possible, to structured care environments and formal education somehow gives them a leg up in life. As it turns out this notion serves the needs of parents instead of serving the needs of their children.

This newer method of dealing with parental regret is easy to *not* notice. Its acceptance has grown and spread over decades until it has now become a norm of the middle class. It became a norm by embedding itself into the existing concepts of education. It is now so well disguised as a positive opportunity, that every parent should strive to provide for their children, that it is difficult to recognize its diabolical purpose and the corrosive effect it has on the children subjected to it. I only became fully aware of ECE's true purpose and its true effect by accident. I noticed that in today's world, there is a unified parental movement to unplug the fantasy life so typical of childhood. This observation forced me to do some extensive research, after which I realized that this movement stems directly from ECE, a sort of collateral effect, if you will. The theory behind ECE advocates the elimination of childhood. Those joyful years once spent learning through playing, experiencing, and exploring, without the intrusion of constant adult supervision, are no more. Instead, those precious years of youth are now spent being incarcerated in the structured environments of ECE facilities, where various forms of formal education are forced down the throats of little children until finally their natural developmental process is strangled to death. To support this process, parents are encouraged to eliminate all childhood fantasies, based on the supposition that such fantasies get in the way of formal education. Parents who buy into this nonsense are telling their children, as young as two or three years old, that Santa Claus is not real. These same parents also have in their crosshairs Santa's elves, Rudolph, Frosty the Snowman, the Easter Bunny, the Tooth Fairy, Peter Pan, and yes, even Tinker Bell. They are also intolerant of their children pretending to be princesses, knights in shining armor, fairy godmothers, or wizards. They are most certainly not accepting of their child having an imaginary friend—so much so that if the child persists, the parents will label their own offspring as "Not Quite Right." To eradicate such childish thinking, adult thinking is forced on children. This is done even though it is obvious that adult thinking is beyond the reach of the child's cerebral development. Children simply do not have the ability to give up fantasies, even if they wanted to. Fantasies are part of an inborn learning program that is essential to the development of the individual. They are critical to a child's early identification of their attributes and of their limitations. It can be said that fantasies are a child's first steps toward self-discovery.

Though these fantasies cannot be given up by children, they can be distorted or damaged by adult interference. In desperation to please adults, children will internalize their fantasies rather than process them through verbalization and role play. When they are forced to do this, the flow of the natural learning process is disrupted. There is a high risk that this disruption will derail the development of fundamental skills, causing the child unnecessary struggles as they grow older. It too creates frustration that results in anxiety. That anxiety can become an internalized anger that changes what should have been fun-filled, whimsical fantasies into dark and violent visions. It is not surprising that many children who find themselves under pressure to conform to their parents' misguided demands act out to vent that internalized anger. Some parents punish children whose acting out is perceived as open rebellion against their authority. That punishment often involves verbal abuse or worse. It commonly includes demeaning the child's intelligence for not being more like an adult's. It is easy to imagine the damage that such harsh criticism does over time. All of this only serves to intensify the anger that the child is experiencing and sets the stage for a very rough road ahead, for both the child and the parents.

The end product of this parental interference with the natural process of childhood development and the negative effects of ECE may be most apparent in the hordes of unsophisticated, socially incompetent students that crowd college campuses and who have become the topic of much academic and political commentary. They are described as well versed, or at least fairly well versed, in book knowledge but incapable of formulating an original thought, even if their very lives depended on it. First-year students arrive on campus equipped with the social skills of a preteen and often present as entitled, defensive, angry, thin-skinned people who overreact to even the most minor slight. Being incessant whiners, they have an uncanny ability to identify or to create problems but possess no ability, perhaps no desire, to solve any problems, even their own. Most spend their first year or more wandering around campus in a clumsy manner searching for a safe haven in a clique, a fraternity, or a social movement. They are known for having no personal identity or direction of their own. Their transient personality traits are the result of mimicking whomever they happen to hook up with, and their direction is often determined by whatever cause has the loudest megaphone. Some, when questioned about personal beliefs, values, or future goals recite the results of high school personality or aptitude tests that were pounded into their heads by mentors and career counselors. Others fumble around for an answer like a person afflicted with expressive aphasia.

Believing that you will get a positive result by stealing your offspring's childhood and replacing it with formal education makes no sense. It makes even less sense when you consider that there is already a natural developmental process in place that is highly efficient if only left undisturbed. All the so-called evidence I have found that attempts to support ECE is provided by those who obviously have skin in the game, and it is blatantly biased. In addition, I have noted that all this "evidence" measures success by superficialities, such as accolades and material gain but never mentions personal growth, becoming a good person, or even being happy. So, I ask you, is it your hope that your child will become an angry, arrogant, emotionally superficial corporate executive with an impressive salary, whose office is decorated in awards and trophies? If so, then incarcerating your little one in an ECE facility as early as possible is definitely the way to go. You will be glad to know that you can start utilizing this socially acceptable method of distancing yourself from your mistake (your baby) when the child is very young. You can deposit infants into typical day cares at six months of age and into a *structured* day care at twelve months. Sounds good, doesn't it? I can imagine many a parent being giddy at the thought of relinquishing much of their parental responsibility to a succession of educational facilities, even if the theory and purpose behind them is dubious. But be warned, that same child who succeeds in the material world may very well turn out to be a self-obsessed, heartless creature, one who will leave you in a cut-rate, dilapidated nursing home to live out your senior years while sitting in your own urine and feces.

If, on the other hand, you are hoping that your child will become a self-assured individual who has their own opinions, beliefs, and values, who knows and pursues their unique purpose in life, who can love themselves as well as others, and who is best known for their good character, then I suggest you think of relinquishing your parental responsibilities to others for what it is—a failure to accept the consequences of your actions. Make a conscious decision to be what you have obligated yourself to be by having a child—a parent. Decide which of you two wage earners is going to quit your job and figure out how to reorganize your priorities and your resources. Then get down to the full-time task of good parenting. Who knows, maybe with a little luck you won't find yourself old and alone in that shabby-ass nursing home, restrained in a Geri-Chair, spending all day wondering if anyone is ever going to come and change that fucking diaper.

PART V

I think that most people understand that meddling with the natural process of development and forcing children into formal education prematurely can turn their little ones into soulless gluttons who are hungry for praise and material gain but void of any positive human characteristics. And it is more than obvious that ECE is only legitimized by opportunists motivated by profit and only supported by decision makers, who are desperate parents themselves, looking for ways to deal with their own parental regret. But parents who should not be parents deny the obvious and have been denying the obvious for some decades. They are so receptive to ECE because it offers them what they want most—freedom to pursue their true ambitions or their pleasures. And what makes this all so enticing is that this freedom can be had in a socially acceptable way, protected under the guise of being a good parent.

This concept of early childhood education did not appear overnight. It floated around for a long time before it landed and took root in American society, sometime in the 1960s. Some say that it began with Jule Sugarman's creation of the Head Start program. Old Jule was a man full of good intention and never dreamed that his concepts on how to help poor and disadvantaged children would end up being used to soothe the guilt of middle-class couples who were determined to detach themselves from parental duties. His ideas were not meant for all children. He designed a summer school program that focused exclusively on helping low-income children, whose developmental process was being impeded by social disadvantages. The program included efforts to support more stable family relationships, enhance the physical as well as the emotional well-being of these children, and provide an opportunity to strengthen their cognitive skills. It proved very successful in helping them catch up with other children by preparing them to start the first grade on a more equal footing. It is important to note that they were only being helped to acquire what other children already had by virtue of being in a stable, nurturing, secure home environment where adequate resources were available to provide for basic needs.

Many people took notice of Sugarman's success, including multiple opportunists. The general concepts surrounding his Head Start program were refashioned, rebranded, and sold as something that all children should be privy to, not just the underprivileged. And it worked. Typical salespeople have always preyed on the gullibility of the common man, but even they were astonished at the willingness of the middle class to buy into the concept of day cares, structured day cares, preschools, and kindergartens. Of course, they did not, at first, understand the underlying motivation. To truly appreciate why the success of ECE was so very astonishing you must assume the perspective of those who originally sold the concept—they were selling *preparatory* school (ECE) to parents whose children were already *prepared*. These children possessed everything that ECE could possibly offer and much more. So, salespeople back then were scratching their heads wondering why was the middle class buying something they already had? What those salespeople eventually learned was that most parents in this world are people who do not want to be parents, which makes them amenable to any opportunity that offers even the slightest hope of being rescued from the eternal neediness of their children.

As is common, one thing leads to another. Forcing ECE on children long before they would have previously been introduced to formal education has led to a disruption of the entire educational system. It resulted in children who were academically overprepared for the first grade. This forced the academic expectations for the first grade to be elevated, which forced the expectations for all the following grade levels (second through twelfth) to increase. So now preschoolers and kindergarteners are performing schoolwork that used to be done by first and second graders, first graders are expected to do the work that used to be assigned to third graders or maybe even fourth graders and so on. Many disadvantaged kids who once benefited from programs like Head Start are again left in the dust by these inflated academic expectations. What a mess our system of education has become. And what a tragedy that childhood should be given up for the sake of having to qualify for some unnecessary and unrealistic entry requirements or to achieve some grossly inflated scores on some random standardized tests. It is sad to think that very soon, perhaps within the next generation, the natural process of childhood development will be all but forgotten in the minds of the middle class. Even the memory of childhood itself will be buried underneath all these new ideas that serve the needs of working parents while disregarding the needs of their children.

PART VI

So here we are—millions of parents producing millions of children that they should have never had. I have described just a few types of parents who fall into this category. The list is much more extensive and includes gambling addicts, drug addicts, alcoholics, religious fanatics, perpetrators of domestic violence, child abusers (of all types), career criminals, persons who suffer from profound and chronic mental illness, persons who are mentally ill but do not yet have a diagnosis such as far-right and far-left extremists, persons who are under the age of consent, persons at the age of consent but who do not possess the sense to know right from wrong, and the list goes on. Our world is on the verge of being overwhelmed by these types of parents and their often dysfunctional offspring. Society's efforts to treat them, support them, and accommodate them has destabilized social order, has nearly emptied the coffers of the state, and has exhausted the patience and generosity of fellow citizens. These folks have hardened the hearts of families, friends, churches, and charities by repeatedly taking advantage of the benevolence of others. Unbelievably they expect, even demand, continued tolerance and, even more unbelievably, they receive it. They receive it from the few innocents left in the world who, like little children, look for the good in everyone and naively believe that these disruptive individuals have the capacity for change, which they do not. It could be argued that some of these parents who do pay taxes make a monetary contribution to society and are therefore entitled to a certain level of tolerance. But the cost that is required to deal with the damage that they and their offspring cause negates any possible financial benefit. And the damage to our society caused by the continued production of these faulty products (damaged children who become damaged adult members of society) is immeasurable and may very well threaten the continuation of the world as we know it in the not-too-distant future.

What's to be done? Well, the truth is there was never any hope for the previous generations of parents who shouldn't have been parents. The same is true of present-day parents who shouldn't be parents. These people simply are what they are, and though they can be many things, they cannot be good parents. Perhaps one or two of these individuals will be touched by Jesus, but short of that, it is impossible for them to suddenly change their core personalities and become something totally different. Most are so delusional, so self-absorbed, or in such profound denial that they have no ability or desire to deal with their parental shortcomings. The harm they have done and are doing cannot be repaired, nor can it be stopped. Typically, the children of these people are also without hope. A few (very few) of these individuals will turn out to be the product of a "lucky" roll of the genetic dice. They will possess a natural ability to rise above their deficient upbringing as well as other adversities they may face in life. But most are irreversibly damaged. They will grow to be adults who never feel good or even comfortable with themselves but never know why. They will never possess the insight to recognize that they are the damaged goods produced by parents who shouldn't have been parents. And, sadly, they will pass that damage along to their children.

Does that mean man's lack of control over a primitive instinct to reproduce, coupled with our outdated social indoctrination, will continue to drag us into a future where bad parenting is the norm? I'm afraid so, at least for a while. Human beings tend to continue down whatever path they find themselves on. They do so because the masses do not possess the mental wherewithal to find a new way. If something is working for them in the moment, they simply ignore any negative consequences and continue on. They only change directions if those negative consequences pile up to the extent that the path they are on is finally blocked and they are forced to take an alternative route. Most often it is the more intellectual persons in our society, those separate and apart from the herd mentality, who must save the common people from themselves. I think that will be true in this case.

PART VII

There is a game changer in the works called genetic engineering. In my imagination, this will be the thing that will rid the world of bad parenting—it may rid the world of parenting altogether. There are bugs to work out and a damaged image that only time can repair. That damaged image is compliments of genetic engineering's predecessor, eugenics, which was popular in the United States (especially in California) in the early twentieth century and emulated by Nazi Germany. Nazis believed in the superiority of the German race and that their race should preserve its purity by selective breeding. It also called for the elimination of lesser races as well as any person with what they considered a mental or physical defect that might contaminate the gene pool. The United States' concept and implementation of eugenics was not very different from that of Nazism. American opinion only turned against eugenics after the media exposed the horrors of the Nazi effort to create their own special version of genetically superior human beings. But those dark memories of the past are fading, and the intriguing possibilities of genetic engineering are enticing us to embrace the future.

I imagine that within four or five decades, all humans will be products of genetic engineering, and they all will be members of a single world society. Each member will be born with a birthmark on their left inner wrist that neatly forms the letters GMH (Genetically Modified Human) and a lot number that identifies the specifics of the genetic material from which that individual is made. It will begin as a privilege of the elite, whose children, after being genetically modified, will become the shining example of what everyone wants their children to be. This privilege will strategically be kept out of the common man's reach for five to ten years to let folks simmer in envy, thereby intensifying the desirability of the product. And then the powers that be will make this technology available to the masses. Within a generation, the planning or implementation of genetic modification will become a common part of every woman's first visit to her obstetrician. Inevitably, the advances in science and technology will make the normal method of human reproduction unnecessary. The only involvement humans may have will be the contribution of genetic material to the global reproduction gene pool if they are chosen as prime donors. All else will be streamlined and managed in a lab. As for those people mentioned earlier who are born to be parents, those with a natural desire to nurture, they will find their place working as staff in world nurseries and parenting centers. Their job will be to assure the successful realization of the specific predispositions that genetic engineering has instilled in each human infant. Lab-based human reproduction will be regulated, based on worldwide data. That data will determine the numbers necessary to guarantee human survival but will prevent excessive population, which would deplete available resources or damage the earth and its atmosphere. To safeguard the preservation of the human species, backup supplies of genetic materials will be securely stored in anticipation of unprecedented population disruptions.

Unlike the early eugenics programs of California and its spawn, Nazi eugenics, there will be no evil intent involved in this futuristic use of genetic engineering. It will have nothing to do with hate. It will have nothing to do with trying to destroy other races or other cultures. The genetic modification of humans will be based on a pure intent to help *all* mankind evolve into something better than what it is. And I do not mean better by the perverse standards of today.

With the change in the method of reproduction, the instinct to reproduce, that force that drives sexual desire, will no longer be necessary. That instinct will be edited out of our DNA. There will be the same variation of distinctive physical features, but physical appearance will no longer be an obsession as it is in the present. Instead, we will come to judge one another first and foremost by the positive features of our character. We will be free from the emotional rollercoaster that we put ourselves on at the beginning of civilization. Back then men mistook or, perhaps, intentionally mislabeled possessiveness for their objects of sexual desire (women) as amore. After all, it does *sound* more noble to kill a rival or to start a war over an object of love than to do so because you're a possessive prick. And women, somehow, mistook the conditional protection that stemmed from that same possessiveness as an act of endearment. Having thus attached these vehement sentiments to their most primitive instincts (reproduction and survival), *Homo sapiens* condemned themselves to live in constant emotional turmoil. What a blessing it will be to be free from all that drama.

In this imagined but very possible future, genetic engineering will not be used to produce super athletes, super warriors who serve as super soldiers, or super aggressive corporate leaders. All GMHs will possess an implanted widget that will prevent assertiveness from ever erupting into actual aggression. In other words, our aggressive nature, having served its usefulness, will be genetically switched off. Violence will come to a quiet end. Physical-contact sports will lose their appeal and be discontinued. There will be no need for armed forces, weaponry, or defense technologies. Corporate leaders, without the aggressive trait, will hone their negotiation skills and learn the value of compromise.

The distribution of intellectual abilities will require only a slight adjustment. There will be no need to create more intellectuals. The ratio of those intellectually gifted to those of high intelligence to those of average intelligence is adequate as it is, though a little tweaking will be necessary when it comes to those who do not ascend to at least the average level. All 85ers (persons with IQs of 85 or less) will, over time, be genetically weeded out so that idiocy does not threaten the tranquility of this new nirvana. Cognitive deficits, addictions of all kinds, poor impulse control, and a multitude of other genetically influenced disorders will be eliminated by way of gene editing. The global society will be free of the immeasurable cost and harm that such abnormalities cause.

It is hard to imagine a peaceful world that supports the advancement of all its peoples, but this and so much more is possible. For this to happen, the power to make global decisions will have to be extracted from the black-hearted, mentally limited, self-absorbed political leaders, whom we now foolishly entrust with our futures. And this will happen, but in the most passive of ways, as genetic engineering slices and dices from the global gene pool any traits that contribute to the future creation of such evil characters. We will have to be led into this future, not by any one individual but rather by a compassionate social consciousness. That consciousness will care not so much about the simple survival of the human species but rather the survival of better human beings living in a better world. It cannot come to pass if our society continues to tolerate and accommodate delinquent parents who, instead of enhancing the general character of our population, only pollute it with the products of their irresponsible parental behaviors and undesirable genetic traits. Genetic engineering, once implemented across the board, will produce an entire world population whose number one concern will be maintaining the quality of the human species. And because of that engineering, the population will have the necessary focus, talents, and intellectual abilities to assure that such quality is maintained.

Some may say that such a future denies people their freedom of choice, but who of us with even the slightest insight believes that such a freedom exists or has ever existed? Are we all not products of a unique sequence of DNA that presents itself as particular predispositions whose realization or lack thereof is influenced by our randomly designated social environment? Are any of us really what we would choose to be if we had a choice? We can all easily observe the sad creatures that mankind has become by simply looking at the endless 24/7 news or into the mirror. Do we really think any intelligent being would be so self-absorbed, so inclined to violence, so lacking in compassion, and so void of basic common sense if he really had a choice?

I wonder if we really have a choice about genetic engineering or the future society that it may create. Is it an inevitability, another stage of mankind's evolution that is just meant to be? Let's hope so. But even if, somehow, we had to choose and were presented with the chance to escape this violent chaos that is our present reality, wouldn't we take it? Wouldn't we voluntarily enter a tranquil existence that offers the possibility of personal fulfillment and contentment, even if it is the product of genetic engineering? I think only the most doltish among us would refuse such an opportunity.

CONCLUSION

As I indicated earlier, there is no help, no clean escape for present-day parents who should not be parents or those millions of clueless and defective offspring that they are mindlessly producing. But there is hope for the grandchildren and great-grandchildren of these folks. The few intellectuals in our midst have been blessed with the mental capacity to conceptualize the science behind and the technology necessary for the realization of genetic engineering. This is likely the greatest, possibly the only, hope for saving future generations from being caught in the parent trap. It also may be mankind's only chance to save itself from the hordes of children growing into the types of adults who threaten the social structure by adding to the social burden. It will require that reproduction and parenting be taken out of the incompetent hands of humans and given over to a technology that has the capacity to produce a morally decent human being who is able to actively contribute to society.

All this talk of a future that eliminates the responsibility of raising children must sound like heaven to those parents who are presently plagued with parental regret. It's too bad they won't be around to enjoy it. I have little to offer them in the way of hope. If by some miracle, the human reproductive instinct subsided and social indoctrination paused long enough for the fog to clear and the world, in one great pleading voice, asked for my sage advice it would be as follows: "For those of you who are not yet entangled in the parent trap, and who know that you are potentially not a 'good parent' as described at the start of this essay, I say to you—*Go!*—in the most expeditious manner, using all available resources to have those fallopian tubes tied and those vas deferens clipped. If you have already been snared, then at least try to save your offspring from suffering your fate. Save them before they are hypnotized by the siren song of reproduction. Do not impose our traditional indoctrination that encourages parenthood.

Stress the perils of submitting to their sexual urges without protection by accentuating the true cost in time, energy, money, and ambitions that reproduction can have on their lives and the lives of their partners. Emphasize, again and again, the multitude of exciting options available in this modern world other than parenthood. School them on all proven birth control options and be sure that these options are immediately and easily accessible. Go as far as to encourage regular and frequent masturbation in hope this will temper their sexual desires and, at least, decrease the possibility of reckless sexual encounters with reckless partners. Almost anything is justified to offer your child a life of their choice, not one chosen by a primitive sexual drive and a socialization rooted in archaic beliefs."

It is unfortunate, but this advice is not likely to reach the ear of any who will have the ability to apply it. Most who are in that trap have settled into some dysfunctional way of life that numbs their distress. They are deaf to advice and blind to any possible escape for themselves or their children. But there are those who simply cannot find a way to live with their parental regret, and they are the ones who struggle and suffer the most. If you are one of those people, you have realized that all hope of having the life you once dreamed of is being crushed by the weight of your parental responsibility. You have tried desperately to figure out a way to make it all work. But that requires being able to concentrate long enough to put two thoughts together, which is impossible in your chaotic world.

Your life is like a personal hell with demonic mini-me's (your offspring) tormenting you day and night. In fact, day and night no longer exist—it has all become just one endless stream of meeting the needs and submitting to the demands of others. Your mini masters only allow you the occasional few hours of sleep, which has left you physically exhausted. You get so little rest that sleep deprivation psychosis has become your normal state of consciousness. In that desperate and psychotic state, you have found yourself sitting in your bedroom, with the door locked. In the background you hear the shrieking voices of those little demons who are possessed by an incessant need for nurturing. That need drives them to hunt you down so that they can suckle the very life out of you. Their voices grate away on your composure, leaving your nerves raw. You find yourself pulling out your own hair by the roots and by the handful, letting the pain distract you from your reality. Your teeth are clenched, tears flow while you hold back a primal scream that you are afraid to release because you fear the rage that might follow. The kids, having sniffed you out, are violently beating on the door. You wipe away the snot that has run down on your lips while whispering to yourself, "There *is* a way to get out of this trap; there *is* a way to escape this hell," as you load shiny brass-coated bullets into a Smith & Wesson revolver. The sound of the gun going off is so loud that it reverberates through the bedroom door, through the house, and through the neighborhood. It is the signal that one parent has successfully escaped the trap. Everyone and everything are quiet for a moment—a silent acknowledgment of that escape. Even the kids get the message. They eventually wander over to the neighbor's house in search of someone else they can suck the life out of.

Alien

Sometimes I think that you can be so lost that you don't know you're lost. The only indication that you're lost is a nagging feeling that something is just not right. That feeling is often all mixed up with recurring longings to be *somewhere*; where, you do not know, but you do know that it is not here.

I have spent my life as a transient in a constant but futile search for that somewhere. But since I have become a sexagenarian, these feelings have evolved. I have become acutely aware that I am in a container looking out through my eye sockets, like an inmate looking out through the slot of his cell door. This awareness has convinced me that my body, this physical structure that surrounds me, is really a prison. Those turbulent feelings that once drove my search for that *somewhere*, which is nowhere here on earth, turned out to be the typical restlessness common among all incarcerated souls. More and more I am sure that my entire existence in this world has been a sentence that I must serve before I can be released and finally head home.

Did I do some wrong, commit some crime that justifies my confinement? I guess I won't know until I get out and back to where I came from. Thank goodness I can now smell freedom, as if it is very near. I've noticed that when I push on my prison door or stretch myself against the walls of this container, there is a little give. I am confident that this old structure has deteriorated with age. Just a little more weakening of the walls or just a little more exertion of my determination to be free, and I think it will crumble.

Just Thinking

****

G+SSc+UO=I

(Genetics + Specific Subculture + Utilized Opportunities = Individual)

****

The degree of our genetic deprivation is directly related to our level of achievable aspiration. One cannot surpass the limitations of their genetic composition.

****

Isn't free will really about a test of our ability to resist doing what we naturally would do? What we would naturally do is referred to as evil and is controlled exclusively by our social programming. When we repeatedly commit evil, it is always related to programming that initially failed or that was originally successful but has become impaired or outright broken. The extent of the evil committed is a reflection of how faulty one's original programming was or how impaired it has become.

****

Doesn't man create his own problems, but then seem surprised when circumstance forces him to face them? Doesn't he then praise himself when he solves those self-created problems, all the while creating more problems? Doesn't it seem like a self-perpetuating process that will end when man finally creates that one big problem that he cannot solve?

****

Man's nature is always corrupt and is usually disguised. But the really unsettling thing is that we repeatedly fool others and others fool us using the same disguises over and over again.

****

Selfishness is the essence of being human. Without it, no acts of evil would be committed, nor any good achieved. We cannot change our essence. Our job is to be sure that the good we achieve outweighs the evil we commit.

****

Our intellect, our most prized possession, that we thank God for giving us, is the thing that is taking us further and further away from him.

****

The people in this world who seem to have the least purpose have in fact the greatest purpose of all—to give others purpose.

****

Is the term Love a romanticized misrepresentation of our instinctual inclination to mate for the sake of species preservation and to seek companionship in our effort to relieve ourselves of our intrinsic loneliness?

****

Unconditional Love creates a beast named Entitlement.

****

A lot of people could become rich simply by not wanting unnecessary shit.

****

Man's ability to produce memories, combined with his ability to communicate through language, enabled him to develop the illusion of time. Before we were able to label seasons, name months, and number years, did we have a past or a future, or was it just the moment and nothing more? Isn't it still?

****

The hallucination that we designate as the present is wedged between two illusions, the past and the future.

****

At some point, it is no longer about the struggle to hold on but rather about the struggle to let go.

****

I guess it's okay to be afraid of dying, but you should ***really*** be afraid of living too long.

****

If you tell someone that you are suicidal, then you probably are not suicidal. You may just need to be saved from something inside yourself. A successful suicide plan is dependent upon "not" telling anyone about your suicidal intent. Failure to keep your thoughts to yourself will most assuredly result in some meddlesome do-gooder disrupting the plan and preventing you from reaching your goal.

****

Food for Thought (Chicken)

It is a comfort food that reminds me of Sunday dinners, holidays, picnics, road trips, family, and friends. Those fond memories, so calming and reassuring, are the root cause of the most despicable violence—the mass murder of hundreds, nay thousands of defenseless, feathered fowl. It is a sad tale of the horrific abuse and suffering of one creature in order to provide for the comfort needs of another. I admit I am a glutton wallowing in self-pity, attempting to fill a bottomless void left by what was but is no more. The pain of that loss blinds me to the vast destruction of life that my self-pity demands. My need for chicken has resulted in the merciless slaughter of so many innocent victims, but still I consumed each one without guilt and with the greatest of delight. My disregard for their lives and their suffering is unjustifiable—unforgiveable. High-pitched clucking and sharp trills fill the air as feathers fly, necks are wrung, and heads severed. Victims are dismembered, disemboweled, boiled or baked whole, some hacked into parts to be fried or grilled. Some have the flesh ripped from their corpse in hunks to be shredded then simmered in a sweet and spicy marinade and served with a Southern-style slaw. I am sure that every *Gallus domesticus* trembles at the thought of me, and if they could tell tales, I am sure I would be the monster in their most often told horror story. All of this for the sake of comfort food, which has only the fleeting power to remind me that I was once loved. You would think after all this carnage, this consumption of countless carcasses, my self-pity would be saturated, that I would have lost my taste for it all. But no, I can honestly say that even now: I have never met a chicken I didn't like.

Acknowledgments

The person most deserving of acknowledgment is my wife, Esther Pauline Cooper. My affection for her runs deep, and my respect for her is immeasurable. She is a constant source of support and has made not only the completion and publication of this book possible but was also key in the publication of two previous books. She was my sounding board for *I Feel, Therefore I Am*, a memoir, and co-authored *The Adventures of Zac and Kat*, a children's picture book. She has my everlasting gratitude for helping me make my dreams come true.

Thank you to Judi Heidel of Perfectly Clear Editing Services. Judi helped my wife and me with this book as well as with the two previous publications. Her ability to identify a contradiction or a weakness in sentence structure, word choice, or content is impressive. What has been most valuable to me is her willingness to invest herself so fully in her work by taking the time to offer input at critical points along the way.

This is the first time I have worked with Ghislain Viau of Creative Publishing Book Design. I have been very pleased. After just a few conversations via email, he designed a cover that truly complements both the title and the content of my book. He also did an amazing job formatting the interior of the print book and the eBook. Thank you, Ghislain, for your endless patience and help with getting the manuscript ready for publication.

And lastly, my profound thanks to Jill Diane Twist. When I needed someone at the last minute to step in to copyedit, proofread, and put the finishing touches on this manuscript, Jill agreed to make time in her busy schedule to get the job done. I am extremely grateful to have been able to work with such a professional and meticulous editor.

www.ingramcontent.com/pod-product-compliance
Lightning Source LLC
Chambersburg PA
CBHW030958210726
48290CB00007B/2373
9781735560038